3

Morandi

"in mortem"

Museo Novecento Firenze

Exit Morandi

edited by
Maria Cristina Bandera
Sergio Risaliti

FORMA

Exit Morandi

°

Il mio sbigottimento alla notizia della morte di Giorgio Morandi non è quasi tanto per la cessazione fisica dell'uomo, quanto è più per la irrevocabile, disperata certezza che la sua opera resti interrotta, non continui; e proprio quando più ce ne sarebbe bisogno. Non ci saranno altri, nuovi dipinti di Morandi: questo è, per me, il pensiero più straziante.

E tanto più se ricordo quel che ancora pochi giorni fa egli mi diceva: – "Se sapesse, Longhi, quanta voglia ho di lavorare.. – ed anche: – "Ho delle nuove idee che vorrei svolgere..."

Parole che mostrano l'improprietà, pur molto diffusa, di assimilare il percorso di un artista, soprattutto se anziano, a una parabola. Nella costante lucidità di Morandi, esso fu piuttosto una traiettoria ben tesa, una lunga strada; speriamo che resti aperta.

°

come ebbi a chiamarla presentandone la mostra al "Fiore" di Firenze il giorno della liberazione di Bologna (e non sapevamo ancora reciprocamente se si fosse vivi o morti ~~se Morandi fosse ancor vivo ed egli sapeva altrettanto poco di noi~~), egli andava conducendo una così poetica ricognizione del mondo di natura da non trovar pari nel cinquantennio che gli toccò attraversare con la sua ombra austera di austero viandante, la cui "vox clamantis" si spandeva anche nelle plaghe più desertiche dell'arte che gli fu contemporanea.

Quelle poche frasi, sussurratemi nei suoi giorni ultimi (ed altre ne riporteranno certamente gli amici più vicini), stupiranno i molti che in Italia hanno lungamente creduto a una certa immobile comodità della posizione di Morandi dinnanzi ai suoi semplici oggetti, disposti, scalati, variati permutati; senza intendere che nella sua lunga, instancabile, solenne elegia luminosa, egli andava conducendo una così poetica ricognizione del mondo da non trovar pari nel cinquantennio che gli toccò attraversare con la sua ombra densa di alto, austero viandante la cui voce di clamante si spanda anche nelle molte plaghe desertiche dell'arte che gli fu contemporanea.

Voglio dire che la statura di Morandi potrà e dovrà crescere ancora, dopo che quell'ultimo cinquantennio sarà stato equamente ridimensionato, ridotto ai suoi limiti e, dove occorra, persino estromesso dal concerto di una storia che possa dirsi civile e cioè in grado d'intendere ciò che di umano sempre si esprime nell'atto dell'artista.

Nulla anzi, più della morte di Morandi, può stimolare a quell'opera di ridimensionamento; dopo la quale ben pochi resteranno a contarsi, forse sulle dita di una sola mano; e Morandi non sarà secondo a nessuno.

Roberto Longhi

Roberto Longhi, Alba 1890 - Firenze 1970.
Exit Morandi, 1964,
ink on cardboard, 310 × 232 mm
Courtesy Fondazione di Studi
di Storia dell'Arte Roberto Longhi, Firenze

Roberto Longhi, Alba 1890 - Firenze 1970.
Exit Morandi, June 1964,
ink on paper, 210 × 156 mm
Courtesy Fondazione di Studi
di Storia dell'Arte Roberto Longhi, Firenze

Giorgio Morandi. Gazing upon the immediate

Sergio Risaliti

Artistic Director
Museo Novecento

Even in as simple a subject, a great painter can achieve a majesty of vision and an intensity of feeling to which we immediately respond.
Giorgio Morandi

The day after Giorgio Morandi's death, a visibly upset Roberto Longhi, a close friend of the artist for "over thirty years" and his greatest interpreter, read out a text for the television programme "L'Approdo". The outdated black and white footage shows the scholar dressed with sober elegance but standing casually on the threshold of what is now the Fondazione Roberto Longhi; behind him, an oleander plant adorned the sun-drenched plasterwork of Villa Il Tasso. *Exit Morandi* left a mark on subsequent history and art criticism. Longhi, who had already talked at an earlier time of "austere luminous elegy" with regard to the "still, silent painting" of Morandi, emphasized a coincidence which, in his view, had epochal consequences: "A capricious but not meaningless nemesis has decreed that Morandi should make his exit on the very day on which the products of 'Pop Art' went on display in Venice." The critic was convinced that Morandi's stature and influence would grow enormously, while the values of the seasonal artistic products commercialized before and after Morandi would be reappraised. Longhi's view, in a world highly receptive to changing tastes and consumerism, might have seemed to be that of a rather reactionary and conservative critic clinging on in defence of a Western tradition of painting linking the world of Giotto, Masaccio, Piero della Francesca, Bellini, and Titian with that of Chardin and Corot, Renoir and Cézanne, culminating in Morandi, the "austere wayfarer whose *vox clamanti* reached even the most arid regions of the art that was contemporary to him". On the other hand, it was a period marked by bold avant-garde movements that thought it possible to annul history in the name of ready-mades and popular or commercial icons (like Warhol's *Brillo Box* or *Marilyn*). Over the course of time Longhi's prediction was borne out, not so much in terms of a subsequent downplaying of Pop Art's radical importance, but more in his pointing to Morandi as a beacon and point of reference for many contemporary artists in tune with the deep and recurrent values of art history, to which the Bolognese painter felt he belonged in producing his universal, silent poems. Morandi's extreme art, the source of a sentimental education, had been discovered by Longhi in 1934, the year of the "scandalous" inaugural lecture at the University of Bologna. In 1945, Longhi wrote some further splendid notes about a group of selected paintings from the period between 1919 and 1943, at a time when Bologna was being freed from Nazi-fascist hold.

Two decades later, in introducing Morandi's solo show at the Venice Biennale in 1966, when the artist had already been dead two years, Longhi enlarged their lasting and profound understanding: "We were, with a difference of just a few months, from the exact same generation, but our closeness (though it did not lead us to depart from using the polite nineteenth-century *lei* form) was wholly mental and was reflected in a harmony of historic preferences that I have never found to such an extent in any contemporary critic. To better understand the modern Morandi, I used to like asking him about the ancients." Morandi was a kind of reverse telescope employed by Longhi's keen eye to scrutinize from afar the course of art history through to the present. Rereading that text today, perhaps the most important passage is not philological in nature but relates to general criticism. In it, Longhi explains what the dividing line was for an artist who rejected any form or expression in which "he saw even the slightest whiff of eloquence, turgidity, agitation, rhetoric, physical violence, titanic force, arrogance or such like. Perhaps because he sensed the consequences from far off." Obviously Morandi was not fond of Botticelli, Pollaiolo, Michelangelo, a certain "misunderstood Primitivism and

Francesco Arcangeli in the mid-1950s.
Courtesy Fondazione di Studi di Storia dell'Arte Roberto Longhi, Firenze

wild Futurism". This was because Morandi, "the monk in his cell" as Longhi immortalized him, built by "digging within and through form, and by layering tonal 'remembrances' in order to come out into the light of the most whole and pure sentiment". Longhi grasped that Morandi was perhaps the last painter endowed with a poetic sentiment, as deep as it was vast, of the mystery of things; his were just a few "useless objects, drab landscapes, seasonal flowers", contemplated as pure forms with the eyes of a conceptual artist who knows that painting is an affair of the mind.

Morandi's world is one in which the subjects are reduced to the essential in order to tick over, minimally. That is why his art looks to us like extreme action, when, having reached the end of a path that others would have taken into abstraction, it stops without retreating, having always chosen a kind of pictorial gnosis which, by extracting motionless truth from reality, reaches the point of perpetuating the image of an object in the constant sentimental variations of colour-form. According to Longhi, Morandi chose very ordinary subjects in order to poetically tell the truth: isolated from the rapid flow of time and from the chaos of the world, objects and places are, in the artist's hands, "necessary symbols, words sufficient to avoid the shoals of abstractionism." They included domestic objects, items with affective value and landscapes contemplated from the window, so humble and modest as to appear remissive to a metaphysical language to which the light of immortality is slowly restored – an image becoming an event in the instant in which mimesis declines and turns blind. We might say, with Massimo Recalcati, that Morandi "paints the object not in order to double its existence in the virtuality of its representation, but to show how its immanence encapsulates a transcendence that eludes any possible representation… he does not limit himself to painting the visible reality of the object, but, by insisting on painting the visible object, he ends up de-realizing it, to make it a witness of the invisible: the image can never be translated into one or more meanings; instead, it is a question of emphasizing its eccentricity with respect to the plane of signification itself. The image that comes in place of the inexpressible signals its convergence with the real: the image does not cover the real, but is the index of the real."

Visiting Morandi's home-studio, Cesare Brandi also found the same ordinary, dusty objects, and noted that their strategic arrangement gave rise to "unexpected windows on the mind". He looked at them as a child does the figures of an open-air puppet theatre, and those things appeared to him as if they were "puppets stuck in a corner by the ferocious Mangiafuoco". The Colombina bottle, the blue and yellow ball "possibly picked up from a lawn, left behind by some playing child, the jar that used to hold coffee, or the wooden board the alarm clock once stood on". Brandi did not miss the element of force – powerful and resistant – in Morandi's poetics, his very singular and absolute way of maintaining the figurative being of a thing right on the cusp of no longer existing, like when an abstract language reaches the point of occupying the whole space of the painting. For Brandi, everything depends on colour, which, while abstracting the visible from the dependence of the thing, revives the object that remains on the field to defend the final vestige of some figurative form recognizable to us, a mirror image or reflection of the world in which we live. In this regard, Brandi speaks of "position colour", which is a substantive quality of the space occupied by a form and not of the object, "so the object as such might and might not be, might be present or absent, near or distant, absent without the object becoming ab-

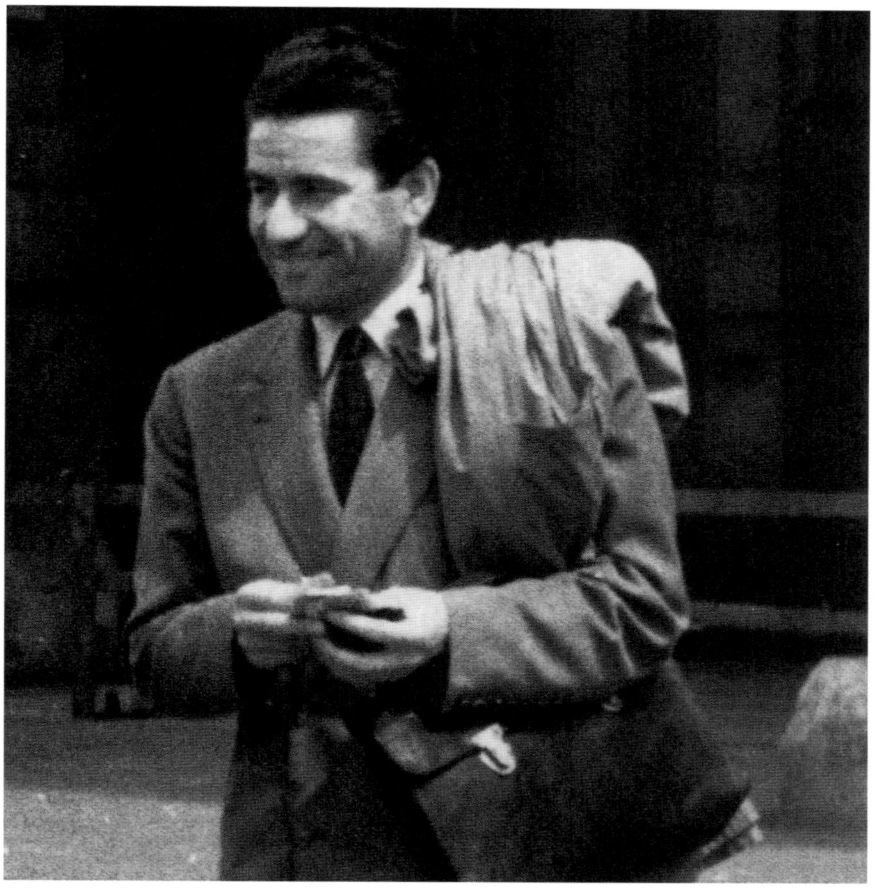

stract. The object can thus remain evident and unreachable even if offered up close to hand". It is perhaps this dual action, on language and sense, that makes Morandi a point of reference for many contemporary artists. Yves Bonnefoy argues that experiencing Morandi is "an entirely different experience from that of his contemporaries, who discerned the illusions of discourse and concluded that they needed to be deconstructed. His experience and his question in any case was this: in the illusoriness of discourse, how is it possible to cling to sense, to maintain contact between words and the world, how, might we say, can they be enabled to create a world? That Morandi posed this question is evident. His figures can only be perceived as vestiges of life, in the silence of ruins, but their colour has preserved an intensity that demonstrates that contact has not been broken with what, in this void, is perceived as being: the flowers are cut, yet they do not fade. And can we not say that the bouquet on that silent table is something that has been placed there? Put there in the expectancy of an arrival?" The French poet and philosopher affirms that, for Morandi, "the constructions of language are only devices for producing illusions [...] that words have no capacity to open up a path to something different from what they are; they have no attitude of truth outside of language, where we have in any case to live, mortal beings that we are. He held that there only therefore remained the possibility of playing with the aspects that words grasp in things: in short, an aesthetic practice, which one should be content with, given that art, this type of art, replaces our existence as vain shadows. While the old landscape painters loved recognizing the place of life, Morandi seems to suggest abstaining from living." At the heart of Morandi's moving pictorial elegy there would thus appear to be an existential mistrust, that he experienced the encounter with reality and life as an experience of absence and emptiness. His work is in fact based on memory and oblivion, as Recalcati sustains: "On one hand [...] it elects the visible – the object in its particular contingency – to be its exclusive centre, but on the other hand it seems to strip this same object of its inevitable transience by elevating it to the dignity of the eternal. Morandi does not just paint the presence of the object, denying its absence: he does the exact opposite. He places presence next to absence, painting, through the presence of the object, its absence, its lostness. And yet in his painting the particular contingency of the object – removed from the erosion of time – becomes an indelible image, an image that remains." A timeless image.

It is worth looking at certain of Morandi's compositions in which the objects are balanced on the edge between the support surface and the surrounding space. Imperilled objects in precarious equilibrium. Yet motionless and resilient. They stand there, and do not fall, by virtue of a harmonious law that stabilizes their presence outside ordinary time and in defiance of the law of gravity. They have a body and a presence that overcome physical laws, as they are forms of a supreme nature, metaphysical images. And in the moment in which we think

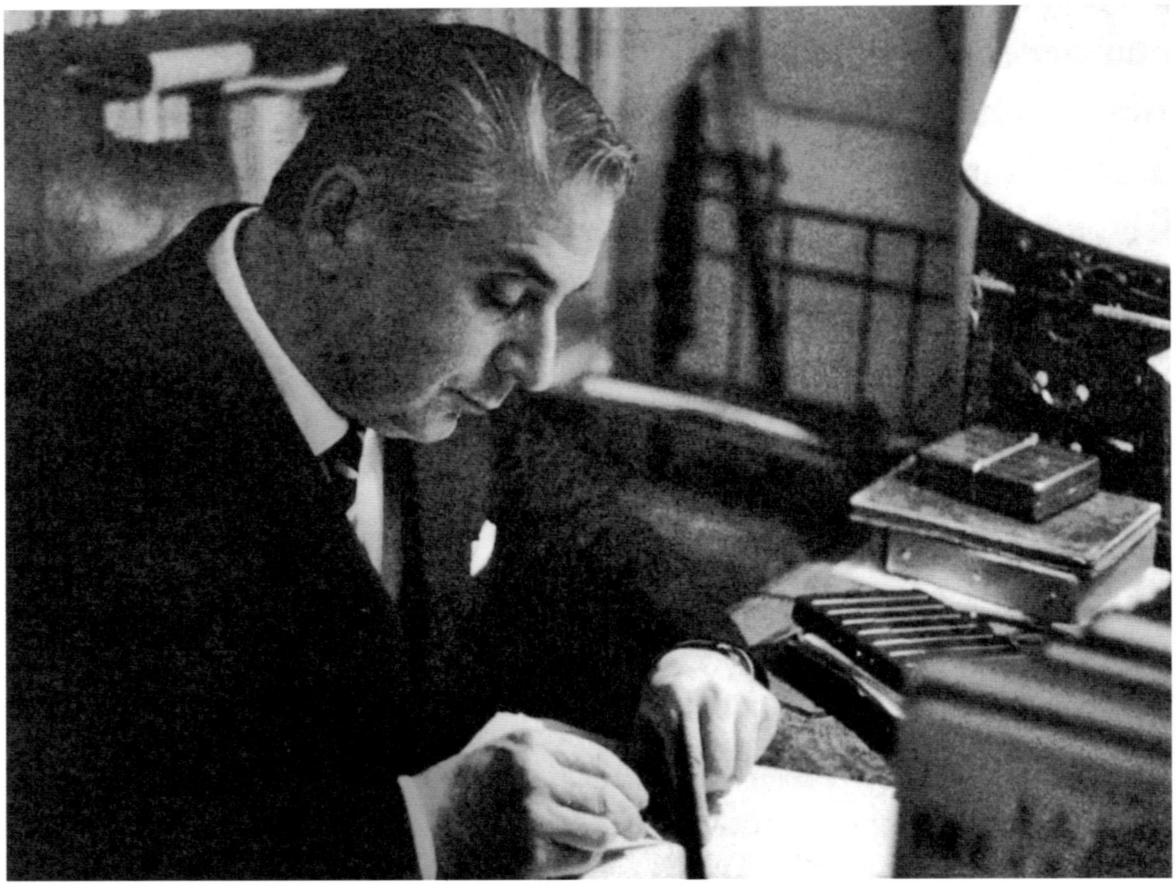

of what is perturbing as the shadow zone of those luminous elegies, we perceive a different sense of life and language coming from colour: "Just when he seems to place the cards of pessimism on the table, Morandi attributes to colour the interiority it owes to light, he lets it speak in the labyrinth of what seemed nothing other than figures; one senses that something substantial is acquiring form once again, thanks to these colours, this time fully and mysteriously revived." The colours thus seem to live a life of their own, once they have been put in a position to construct objects rather than reproduce them. Bonnefoy continues by declaring that "there are, in his still lifes, colours which are close to each other and which at the same time remain distinct. If some blue and brown are side by side, it is not to benefit any intention or thought, it is something as extraneous to networks of meaning as the breaking of sea spray on the sand[...]. Though he perceived the continuity and compactness of sensory appearance in the outside world, he no longer seemed interested in that outside, in that big natural object, when he painted his boxes, his bottles, arranged with care on the table in his studio. Those objects did not count in his life [...] they were nothing other than pretexts for painting, and it is even known that on occasion he applied a clearly distinct colour on one of those objects, anticipating what the picture demanded." Finally, Bonnefoy ends by asking: "What is Morandi's thought? We note above all that [...] the most silent colour reigns everywhere, colour as silence. That colour which is differentiated without dividing passes from one side to the other of the figures, establishing, between the blues and browns, the reds and ochres, relationships that seem to ignore the bottles, the bowl, the painted cup. But despite that, those particular objects are obstinately there in the image, while the painter's art seems instead to exhort us to go beyond them. Instead of dissolving under the influence of a more close-up perception [...] it is as if these figures of things are indicating to Morandi their refusal to abdicate their own being [...] Those bottles and those boxes certainly have a meaning, it is in their being present and absent that one must hope to encounter the painter's thought."

The increased understanding today of Morandi's greatness lies precisely in the way in which he took part in and shaped the course of art in the twentieth century and beyond. He was a shining example both in the way he worked on his pictorial idiom and in his moral stance; his robust faith in silence, his tendency to seclude himself, vigilantly, proceeding towards

Cesare Brandi. Courtesy Polo Museale della Toscana, Pinacoteca Nazionale di Siena, Archivio Cesare Brandi

the mystery of the "thing" illuminated by poetry, without distractions or vacuous curiosity, but always with a steady gaze, focused on materials and values, always concentrating on minimal variations of feeling, in perceiving outlines and gauging colours, which was so crucial, as we have understood, in the construction of the picture-image. It appears clear that the painter imposed on himself a "monk-like" pattern of life and working practice in order to achieve a poetic dimension consisting of humility and force, a sensibility at once receptive and powerful in defining the limits of the event and in attaining the invisible in the immediate. Morandi sought, in the slowness of pictorial touches, to slow down vision until it came to an impossible stop on the thing, so as to contrast, on one hand, the loss of the image's aura, and, on the other, the consuming of the world and of vision. An unstoppable and perhaps irreversible consumption, whereby the "thing" is just a copy. Morandi attended, instead, to the thing and the gaze, saving one from become goods, the other from slipping into reproduction. A heroic and perilous act of the poet in the age of "poverty", according to Heidegger, who wrote about this in relation to the lyrical poetry of R. M. Rilke. "Already during his life", writes Brandi, "he was a classic who miraculously brought his classicism into the historic present, without the need for the step back demanded by the past. His painting had so totally proved victorious that it could allow itself to be different from everything surrounding it and not to be antiquated, and above all never to be in the manner of itself. For this reason, it was as if the painting of Morandi, the living Morandi, had already received the judgment of posterity." Albeit with different approaches and ideas, Francesco Arcangeli and Carlo Ludovico Ragghianti also recognized and appreciated this role of Morandi's, who they interpreted as a totally avant-garde, modernist artist and, at the same time, as profoundly classical. And this was the point of convergence in the judgments of those great art historians: they were, individually and together, fully conscious of the classicism of Morandi, an interpreter and protagonist of a modernism addressed with imperturbable clarity of vision. This forms the basis for a special exhibition project, which brings together works which belonged to or gravitated in the orbit of the four eminent art historians, sealing, in the flow of time and the changing of seasons, their faith in the painting of Giorgio Morandi.

Works consulted

M. Heidegger, *Sentieri interrotti*, La Nuova Italia, Florence, 1996

C. Brandi, *Come un'autobiografia*, edited by V. Rubiu, Edizioni della Cometa, Rome, 1998

C. Brandi, *Morandi*, edited by M. Pasquali, Gli Ori, Pistoia, 2008

R. Longhi, *Da Cimabue a Morandi*, Arnoldo Mondadori Editore, Milan, 2008

Y. Bonnefoy, *Morandi Giacometti e Hollan*, Abscondita, Milan, 2015

M. Recalcati, *Il mistero delle cose. Nove ritratti di artisti*, Feltrinelli, Milan, 2016

Giorgio Morandi. *Natura morta*, 1957 ca.,
V. 1057, oil on canvas, 36.5 × 46.5 cm (detail)
Courtesy Polo Museale della Toscana,
Collezione Cesare Brandi, Vignano

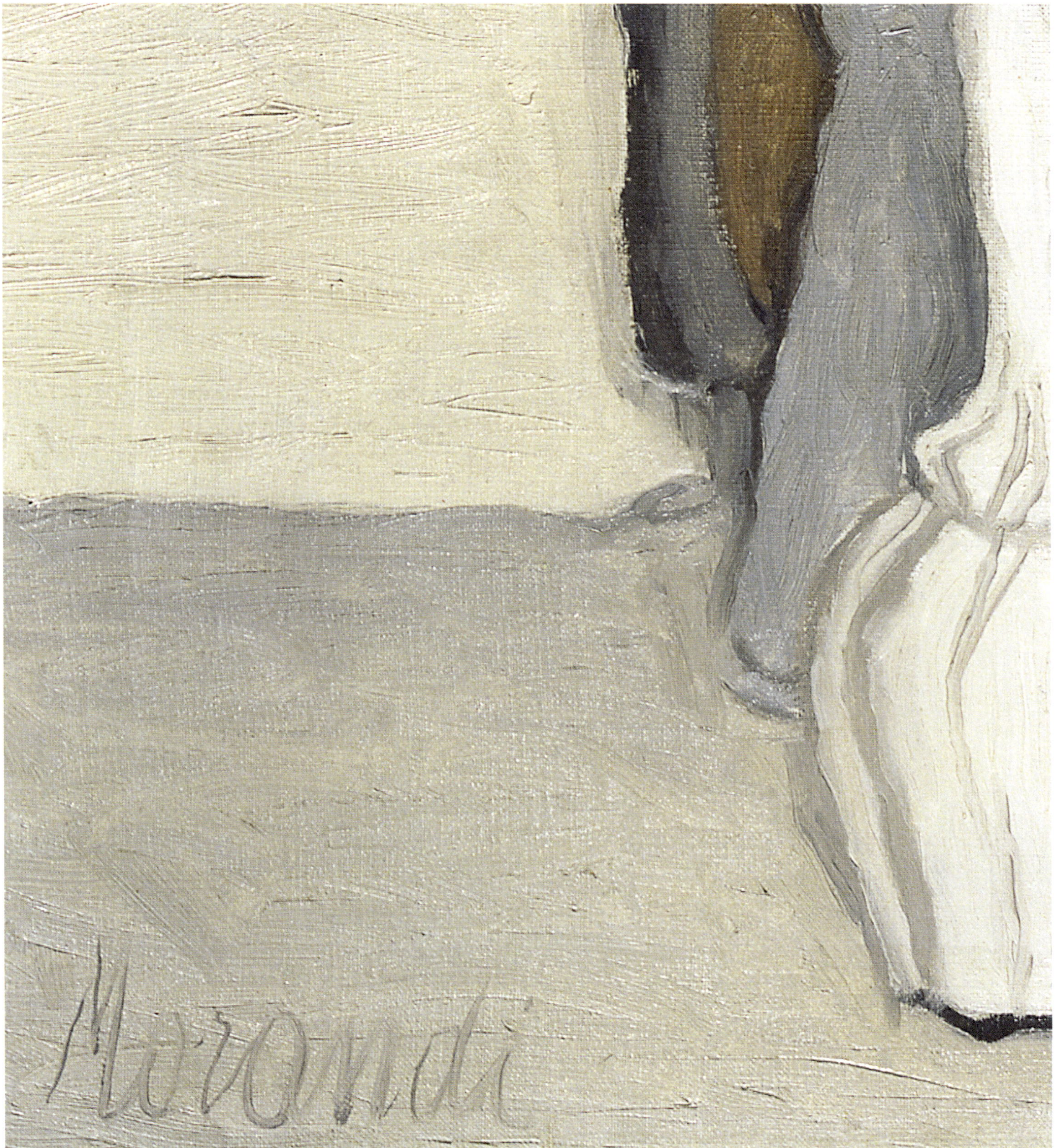
Morandi

Florence, 28 June 1964

Maria Cristina Bandera

Florence, 28 June 1964: "I mean that Morandi's stature can increase further, and must, after the last fifty years have been impartially reconsidered. [...] Nothing, therefore, more than his death, can spur on that reconsideration; after which very few artists will be worth counting, perhaps no more than on the fingers of one hand; and Morandi will be second to none". These authoritative and far-sighted remarks by Roberto Longhi were prophetic, and now stand confirmed by the international and truly boundless interest in the painter. This was not some casual prophecy, but a pondered critical judgment, developed over thirty years, and uttered by the great art historian on the steps leading to his study at the Villa Il Tasso in Florence, before a television camera recording a broadcast of "L'Approdo", scheduled ten days later to commemorate the painter's passing on 18 June 1964. The filmed words,[1] with a hand-written transcript[2] that was later fine-tuned and cropped, losing some of the emotion prompted by the loss of "one of my greatest friends", became a text and was published under the title "Exit Morandi" in *L'Approdo Letterario*.[3]

The camaraderie, based on both intellect and friendship, between Longhi and his contemporary Morandi (both were born in 1890) had begun with another essential assertion made by the former – three decades earlier, in late 1934, during the inaugural lecture given as new chair of the department of History of Art at the University of Bologna, Morandi's own city. The speech was unexpected and it shook his audience, crowded into "a packed lecture-hall",[4] enduring as a milestone of the critical literature on the painter, who until that time (though already in his forties) had only gained the recognition of friends who were artists, men of letters and painters such as Bacchelli, de Chirico, Soffici, Carrà, and Longanesi (who owned the *Natura morta* [Still Life], c. 1929, V. 151, exhibited here[5]). On this occasion Longhi ended his enlightened review of *Momenti della pittura bolognese* with an authoritative accolade, the first Morandi received from the official world of scholarship: "and I conclude by saying that I do not find it entirely accidental that one of the best living painters in Italy, Giorgio Morandi, even today, while steering among the most perilous shoals of modern painting, has nonetheless always succeeded in directing his journey with slow meditation and affectionate studiousness, as if he were a new *incamminato*".[6] As Attilio Bertolucci recalled, it was truly "explosive", since the painter "was considered with suspicion by most of those present, as 'a futurist'".[7] In short, at this point in history, Longhi had immediately recognised Morandi's absolute greatness and above all his unique quality, which was capable at that time of stirring up stagnant water.

A decade later, as we can read in the memorable introductory text of the small, moving one-man show that opened on 21 April 1945 at the Galleria Il Fiore in Florence – newly-liberated but still in ruins after the Second World War – the critic entrusted the painter with the task "of serving as a lesson to the best", when a question still remained: would painting's metaphorical ball "fall into the basket containing the coloured remnants of a more than superficial Romanticism, or into that of the most 'centrist' mental nothingness?".[8]

Years afterwards, with the pressure of criticism dictated by the passing of time, but especially by the evolution of the art world, Longhi defined Morandi as an antidote to "all the deviations of taste for the abstract". This is clear from a passage in the letter he wrote in April 1962 to "Momi", his familiar name for his old pupil Francesco Arcangeli, the former owner of the *Natura morta* [Still life], 1948, V. 612, exhibited here in Florence. Longhi disap-

Ghitta Carell, Roberto Longhi, 1934.
Courtesy Fondazione di Studi di Storia dell'Arte Roberto Longhi, Firenze

proved of the reading of Morandi in Arcangeli's monograph – not published until after the painter's death, the author having earlier failed to receive Morandi's consent,[9] and of which the author had sent him an advance typescript to get an authoritative opinion – and contested the "excessively Bolognese / Italian / European setting" in favour of an interpretation that "admits that Morandi was immediately able to react to, or rather reject, his own environment".[10] It is worth rereading this in order to get a precise sense of the antithesis between Longhi and Arcangeli, insisted upon by the former with his repeated and certainly not random use of the words "for me": "For me, instead, Morandi is a bitter rebuke to all the deviations of taste for the abstract (both Platonic and cosmological-spiritual) that took place between 1910 and 1920. Here our disagreement concerns the very different value judgements the two of us give to modern movements; yours positive, mine basically sceptical and negative (that is, once we have excepted the first Cubists: Klee, and Soutine). All the others, for me, should not be mentioned near Morandi, even tangentially. His phrase 'there is nothing more abstract than the visible world' is the most exalted statement of anti-abstraction ever made".[11]

In this context, and entirely consistent with his earlier point of view, it is hardly surprising that Longhi used Morandi's death as a barrier against the wave of American art that was disseminating itself through the Biennale, underlining in the broadcast eulogy of 1964 (the *Exit Morandi* with which we began) how "a capricious but not entirely meaningless twist of fate has decreed" this should have happened "on the very day the creations of pop art were being spread and exhibited in Venice with pomp and circumstance" [corrected in the written text as just "exhibited in Venice"].[12]

Speaking to the microphone and camera for "L'Approdo", after starting with a voice tinged with emotion for the loss of his friend, Longhi recovered his theatricality and used a contemptuous, recitative tone, with assonances (in Italian) to underline the words expressing his critical dissent: "propalati [...] con grande pompa", "prodotti" and "pop-art". Although this is not the occasion to discuss the divergent opinions of Longhi and Arcangeli, on which much ink has been spilled, especially in the late twentieth century – when people debated whether or not Morandi's painting related to the abstract tendencies of his time, a now well-digested question – we should recall that even the younger and more "aligned" of the two scholars did not fail to emphasise in his troubled biography (its date of writing annotated "July 1960 – December 1961"), how the "fame" of the painter, who for Arcangeli and the friends of his generation was already "now an exalted legend",[13] "was destined to increase throughout the world".[14]

It should however also be remembered that the image that Morandi sought to convey of how he worked – often personally choosing the sequence of pictures in one-man exhibitions[15] – was in tune with Longhi's exegesis. Not adhering to the supremacy of the 'modern', this reading removes Morandi from the contingencies and proximity with the artistic trends of his period (even the international ones), though the painter had a thorough and selective knowledge of them, in order to underline the strongly independent path he had chosen. Morandi's resolute and tenacious awareness of his own oeuvre led him to state, in his *Autobiography* of 1928, how after a formative period in which he meditated on "the work of the old masters, which takes reality as its constant source of inspiration", he had understood "the need to follow my instincts all the way, trusting to my own strength and forgetting any stylis-

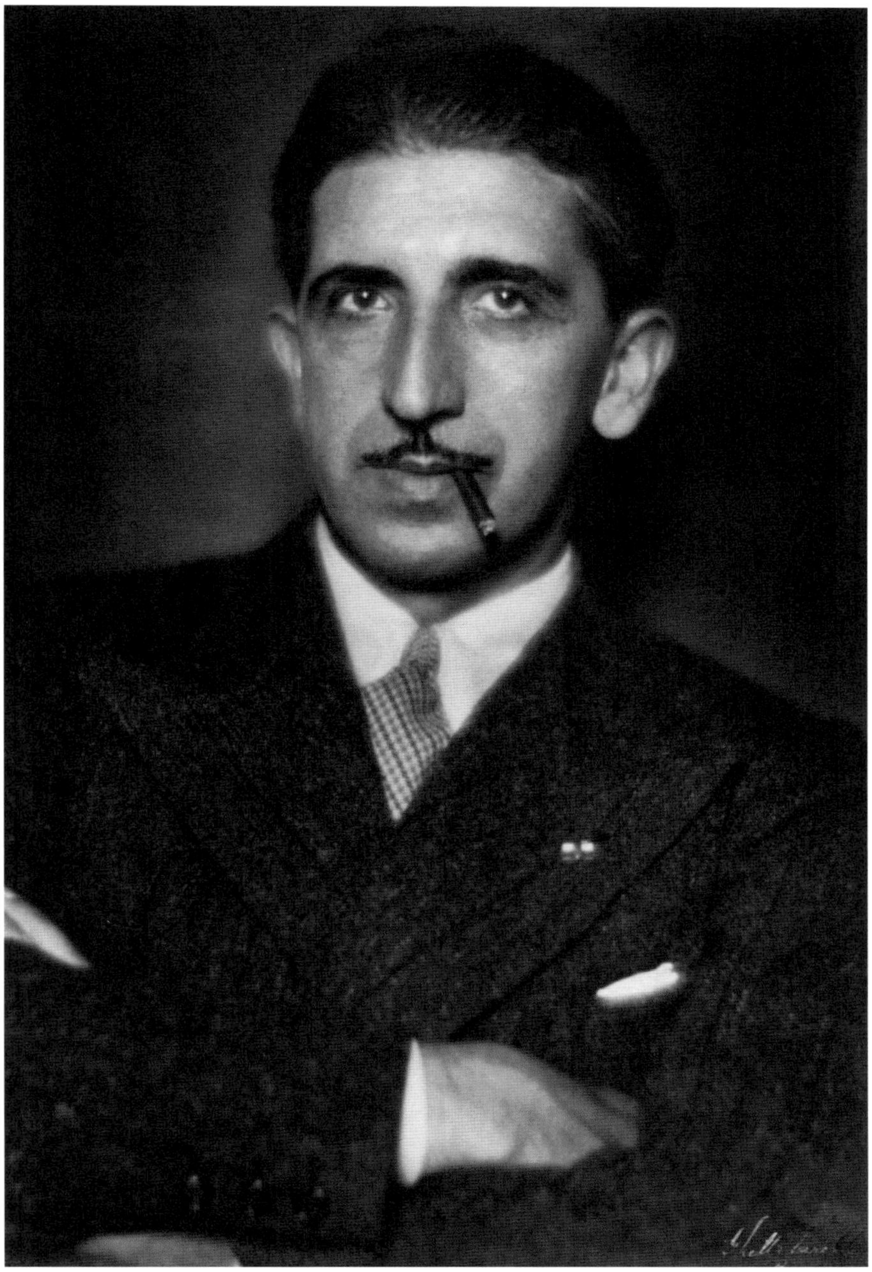

tic preconceptions during my work".[16] A decade later – in a 1937 interview by Piero Bargellini, who in his role as director of the journal *Il Frontespizio* was publishing brief biographies of Italian artists – this independence of thought would prompt him to explain the purpose of his art with these lucid and unhesitating words: "what matters is to touch the limit, the essence of things".[17] This is a central statement of Morandi's poetics. Bargellini followed it with this comment: "He says 'essence' and one feels he means 'being'. Not appearance, but being".[18]

Based on these assumptions, what Longhi says – the result of a thirty-year long "entirely mental intimacy" with Morandi,[19] strengthened by shared artistic values[20] and above all by an powerful mutual admiration that led them never to move away from the use of 'Lei' (the respectful third person, for 'you') in both conversation and correspondence – casts light on our understanding of the painter and his "taut trajectory" and "long road". This was an intense intellectual affinity, made tangible by the words of appreciation they exchanged in letters, concentrated and quite devoid of flattery: "I have just received your etchings – admirable", wrote Longhi in 1938,[21] with reference to the pieces which entered his collection and now exhibited here: *Natura morta (natura morta con la statuina)* [Still Life (still life with the statuette)], 1921, V. inc. 17; *Landscape (View of the church of the Osservanza in Bologna)* [Paesaggio (Veduta dell'Osservanza di Bologna)], 1922, V. inc. 16; *Paesaggio con la ciminiera (Sobborghi di Bologna)* [Landscape with chimney (Suburbs of Bologna)], 1927, V. inc. 27.[22] As for Morandi, he told the art historian in 1951 that "I have already been to the Caravaggio exhibition. Magnificent",[23] referring to the historic show that had recently opened at the Palazzo Reale in Milan.

Addressing the reader in a 1961 foreword to his own *Scritti giovanili* (youthful writings), Longhi used outstanding words of praise: "[Morandi is] still at the cutting edge of modern art today."[24] This statement found an equally pregnant echo in the same year, in a letter from the painter: "I am reading your *Scritti giovanili* – as you can imagine, with keen interest. Like the rest of your writings, these words teach, as they have in the past and will continue to in the future."[25]

This was one of the most intense comradeships ever recorded between an artist and a critic, and as we know, Morandi had on his desk with him until his final days a copy of his mentor's monograph on *Piero della Francesca*, published by *Valori Plastici* in 1927.[26] Its critical stance and wealth of innovative illustrations provided him with a constant stimulus,

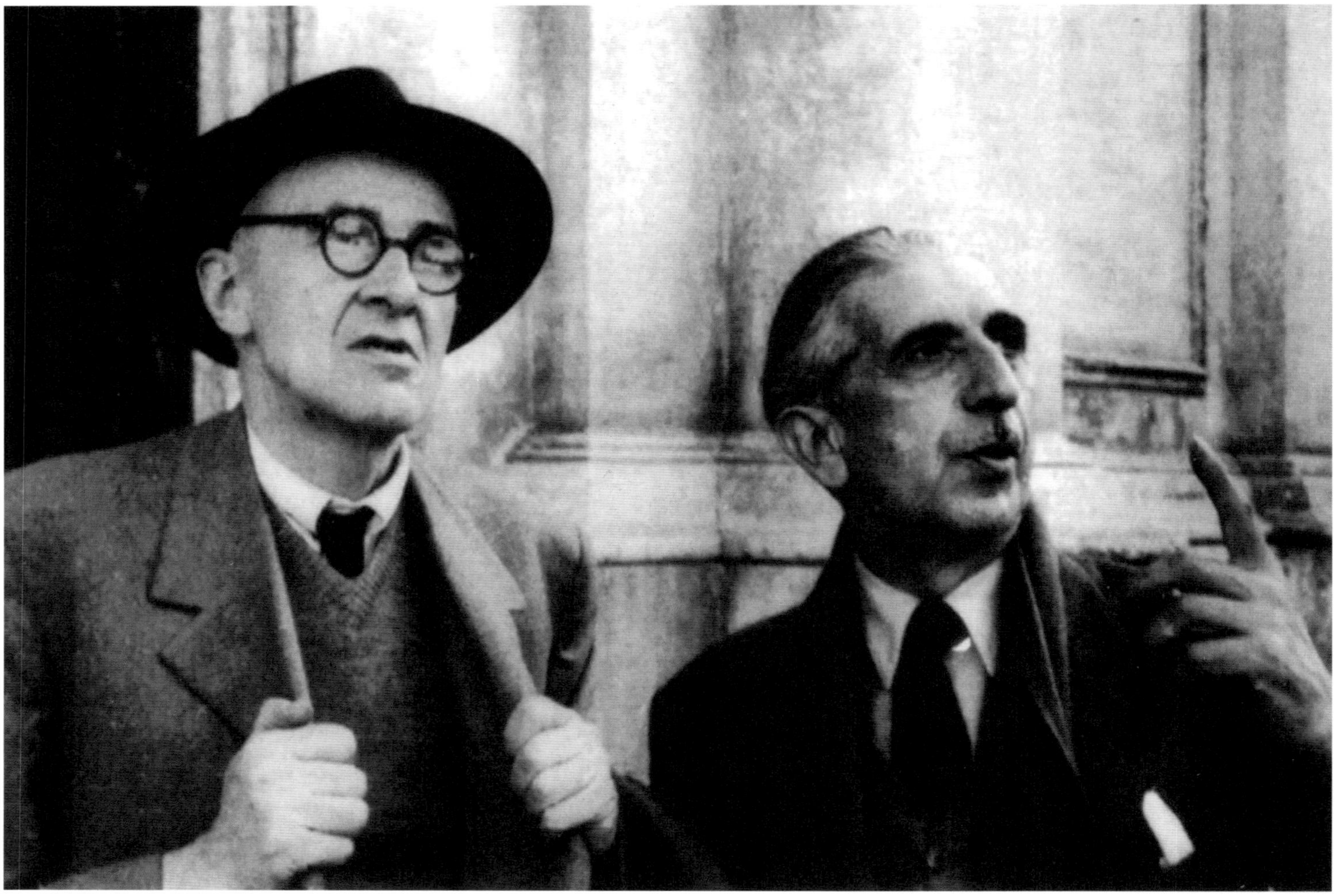

Giorgio Morandi and Roberto Longhi in the 1950s.
Courtesy Fondazione di Studi di Storia dell'Arte
Roberto Longhi, Firenze

which left its mark in many of his works.[27] This is clear, in the present exhibition, in the *Natura morta* [Still Life], 1941, V. 31, in which the protagonist bottle forms hark back to the detail of the turreted cityscape in the background of Piero's *San Gerolamo e un devoto* [Saint Jerome and a supplicant] (c.1458/1460, Venice, Gallerie dell'Accademia).[28] As for Longhi, in 1966, during the posthumous Morandi retrospective organized by the Venice Biennale, he recalled a significant earlier meeting and spoke of the harmony between them, noting that this was "on a level I have never found in any other critic of my age".[29]

These words of Longhi about Morandi are special, especially those of the foreword to the exhibition of twenty-one very carefully selected works at the Fiore gallery in 1945[30] – four of which, owned by Longhi, are exhibited here: *Natura morta in viola* [Still Life in viola], 1937, V. 222; *Paesaggio* [Landscape], 1932, V. 174; *Paesaggio* [Landscape], 1940, V. 277; and *Fiori* [Flowers], 1943, V. 408,[31] together with the later *Natura morta* [Still Life], 1954, V. 906, which now belongs to the Foundation named after the art historian, and the *Paesaggio (Cortile di via Fondazza)* [Landscape (Courtyard in Via Fondazza)], 1935, V. 196, formerly owned by Roberto Longhi, subsequently by his physician, and now in the Merlini collection.[32] These should be understood as evidence of their "elevated affinity",[33] but above all they represent an indispensable support for understanding and penetrating his painting, at the same time revealing Longhi's clear-headedness in capturing its essence.

Longhi's 1945 text presents Morandi in his uniqueness, speaking of his world, his "monk"-like, meditative, thoughtful, and thought-out existence, rather than one that is locked into an "ivory tower", with a meaning that is hard to deconstruct; of his elective affinities, of his simple, subdued and anti-heroic painting, of his reluctance with regard to narrative, of the reflective slowness which Longhi explains by referring to the slow narration of Proust rather than to a comparison with other contemporary artists. Nonetheless, connecting ancient with modern, the critic shares with great clarity a preferential list of painters from a past both distant and close to whom Morandi directed his gaze: "in chronological order: Giotto, Masaccio, Piero, Bellini, Titian, Chardin, Corot, Renoir, Cézanne".[34] Longhi's text underlines how Morandi's peculiar method involved "the reduction of the subject to something that was barely ticking over", the "abolition [...] of an intrusive subject", the avoidance of "importunate" human figures, the absence of mimesis and detail in landscape in favour of "desolate landscapes"[35] – in short, emphasising how his art, with no connotation and devoid of narrative, went beyond the strict bracketing of artistic definition, and above all, beyond the moment.

These words are more relevant than ever, and in their recognition of the absolute quality of Morandi's art, of his painting without titles – but for the anodyne 'still life', 'landscape', or 'flowers' – they find resonance with many artists of our own time, within the broad spectrum of painters, directors and authors, worldwide (suffice it to consider the Chinese artist Zeng Fanzhi, captivated by the "sense of the infinite" of his painting[36]), and observe and interact with him.[37] The list is too long to go into detail, so we shall limit ourselves here to referring the reader to an earlier essay,[38] and mention some representative examples. Among these are the film-maker Tacita Dean, who underlined Morandi's determination to transform his objects, "making them the objects he wanted to see", rather than exclude what it was about an object that he did not deem necessary"[39]; Tony Cragg, who noted that "the world would be a much poorer place without his work"[40]; Bernard and Hilla Becher, captivated by his respect for things, by "the very way in which he selected and organized his typical objects at the centre of the image, turning them into basic compositional elements"[41]; Lawrence Carroll, charmed by Morandi's choices: "What an extraordinary example and gift he is to us, a painter who follows in his spirit of painting, one that he adopted from those who came before him [...] he now has passed on his life's example to future generations",[42] and "one does not need to look far for what is important. One does not need to abandon oneself. One does not need to follow fashion [...]. One simply needs to trust deeply what one has"[43]; and Rachel Whiteread, whose small-scale works set in the rooms of the Museo Morandi established a silent, subtle and refined conversation with the painter.[44]

We should add literary figures to this list, for their sharp-minded interpretations of Morandi: Pier Paolo Pasolini, who speaks to us of "the effable"[45] in the evocative painted poetry; Don DeLillo, who dwells on the irregular edges of the objects that fascinate the protagonists of his novel *Falling Man*[46]; Paul Auster, who uses his incisive writing to describe paintings that evoke "the mute wonder of pure thingness"[47]; and Siri Hustvedt, who investigates and analyses Morandi's "drama of perception".[48]

In conclusion, for its depth of thought and connection with the past, and for how it keenly opens out towards a reality beyond the present, the last word must go to Bernardo Bertolucci, the late, great master of cinematography – and son of the poet Attilio Bertolucci, himself a pupil of Longhi – who had a "crush" on Morandi, captivated by the "monumentality" of his small canvases and by their "subdued tone". Fascinated by his paintings, he compared them with Borges' short story *The Aleph*. Accustomed to being behind the camera, he revealed in a recorded interview, with great determination – though barely audible, he too with a "subdued tone" – how within these paintings, "apparently so simple, so rigorous, there is always a place from which one catches sight of infinity", a point from which one can see "a huge number of other things in the world, all at the same time".[49]

1 For the broadcast script see M. C. Bandera, "Miscellanea per Morandi", *Paragone,* LVII, 67 (675), May 2006, pp. 43-46.

2 R. Longhi, *Exit Morandi,* manuscript, Florence, AFRL (Archivio Fondazione di Studi di Storia dell'Arte Roberto Longhi), Morandi files: "Exit Morandi".

3 R. Longhi, *Exit Morandi,* remarks for "L'Approdo", television broadcast of 28 June 1964, and printed in L'Approdo letterario, X, 26 April – June 1964, pp. 3-4, now in idem, *Scritti sull'Otto e Novecento 1925-1966 (Opere complete, XIV),* Florence, 1984 pp. 215-216.

4 As recalled by his pupil from that time, Francesco Arcangeli (*Giorgio Morandi,* 1964, p. 277), who had taken his place in the back of the room and lamented that he had not been close enough to witness the almost astonished surprise of those in the front rows.

5 The initial "V." followed by a number refers to the general catalogue of painting and their corresponding listing: L. Vitali, *Morandi. Catalogo generale,* Electa, Milan, 1977, 2 vols. (2nd expanded ed., 1983).

6 R. Longhi, "Momenti della pittura bolognese", *L'Archiginnasio,* 1-3, 1935, p. 135, reprinted in idem, *Da Cimabue a Morandi. Saggi di storia della pittura italiana scelti e ordinati da Gianfranco Contini,* Milan, 1973, p. 217. The play on words at the end refers to the Accademia degli Incamminati ('Academy of the Progressives'), founded by the Carracci in the 1580s.

7 A. Bertolucci, "Un maestro esplosivo", *L'Illustrazione Italiana,* December 1962, p. 62.

8 R. Longhi, *Giorgio Morandi,* exhibition catalogue (Florence, Il Fiore Galleria d'arte moderna, 21 April – 3 May 1945), Florence, 1945, p. 12, reprinted with an added *Premessa* (foreword) in *Catalogo della XXXIII Biennale di Venezia,* Venice, 1966, now in R. Longhi, *Scritti sull'Otto e Novecento 1925-1966 (Opere complete XIV),* Florence, 1984, p. 96.

9 F. Arcangeli, *Giorgio Morandi,* Milan 1964, with the foreword "printed on 31 July 1964". On the thorny question of the publication of the monograph, see *Giorgio Morandi di Francesco Arcangeli. Stesura originaria inedita. Introduzione, apparati, note,* ed. by L. Cesari, Umberto Allemandi, Turin, 2007.

10 R. Longhi, in the letter to F. Arcangeli dated 10 April 1962, published by P. Mandelli, "Storia di una monografia", *Accademia Clementina – Atti e Memorie,* no. 35-36, Bologna, 1995-1996, pp. 333-334, and more recently by L. Cesari, "Appendice II. Lettere per una storia editoriale", in *Giorgio Morandi di Francesco Arcangeli,* cit. 2007, p. 664.

11 R. Longhi, *ibidem.*

12 For the recording, see M. C. Bandera,

"Miscellanea per Morandi", cit. 2006, p. 45; for the written text, R. Longhi, *Exit Morandi (1964)*, cit. 1984, p. 216.

13 F. Arcangeli, *Giorgio Morandi,* cit. 1964, p. 289.

14 F. Arcangeli, *Giorgio Morandi,* cit. 1964, p. 338.

15 A prime example is the exhibition organised by the Venice Biennale at the 1957 São Paulo Biennale, where Morandi was awarded the international prize for painting. See M. C. Bandera, *Morandi sceglie Morandi. Corrispondenza con la Biennale 1947-1962,* Charta, Milan, 2001.

16 G. Morandi, in his autobiography: "Giorgio Morandi", in "Autobiografie di scrittori e di artisti", *L'Assalto,* 18 February 1928, in *Giorgio Morandi 1890-1964,* exhibition catalogue (New York, The Metropolitan Museum of Art, 16 September – 14 December 2008; Bologna, MAMbo 22 January – 13 April 2009) ed. by M. C. Bandera and R. Miracco, Skira, Milan, 2008-2009, p. 346.

17 G. Morandi to P. Bargellini, "Artisti italiani: Giorgio Morandi", *Il Frontespizio,* September 1937, now in *Giorgio Morandi 1890-1964,* cit. 2008-2009, p. 348.

18 *Ibidem.*

19 The present writer has addressed the shared experiences and intellectual friendship of Longhi and Morandi on several occasions: M. C. Bandera, "Morandi e Firenze. I suoi amici critici e collezionisti", in *Morandi e Firenze. I suoi amici critici e collezionisti,* exhibition catalogue (Florence, Fondazione di Studi di Storia dell'Arte Roberto Longhi, 21 January – 6 March 2005), ed. by M. C. Bandera, Mazzotta, Milan, 2005; M. C. Bandera, "Longhi e gli amici pittori", in *La collezione di Roberto Longhi dal Duecento a Caravaggio a Morandi,* exhibition catalogue (Alba, Fondazione Ferrero, 14 October 2007 – 10 February 2008), edited by M. Gregori and G. Romano, L'Artistica Editrice, Savigliano (Cuneo), 2007, p. 49; M. C. Bandera, "Morandi will be second to none", in *Giorgio Morandi – Roberto Longhi. Opere Lettere Scritti,* ed. by M. C. Bandera (Quaderni della collezione Merlini, 2), exhibition catalogue (Florence, Fondazione di Studi di Storia dell'Arte Roberto Longhi, 1 – 22 June 2014), Silvana Editoriale, Cinisello Balsamo (Milan) 2014, pp. 151-161.

20 The subject is discussed in F. Fergonzi, "Morandi e i quadri degli altri", in *Filologia del 900 Modigliani Sironi Morandi Martini*, Electa, Milan, 2013, pp. 161-216; M. C. Bandera, "Morandi's Eye. From Giotto to Piero della Francesca, Caravaggio, Zurbarán and Vermeer", in *Morandi infinite variations,* exhibition catalogue (Hyogo, Prefectural Museum of Art, 8 December 2015 – 14 February 2016; Tokyo, Station Gallery, 20 February – 10 April 2016; Iwate Museum, 16 April – 5 June 2016), ed. by L. Selleri and G. Vecchi, Tokyo, 2015, pp. 30-37 and 182-187; *eadem,* "Morandi, Roberto Longhi e gli Old Masters", in *A Backward Glance: Giorgio Morandi and the Old Masters,* exhibition catalogue (Bilbao, Guggenheim Bilbao, 12 April – 6 October 2019) ed. by Petra Joos, in press.

21 R. Longhi to G. Morandi, undated letter but late 1938, Bologna, Archivio Museo Morandi; most recently published in "Giorgio Morandi – Roberto Longhi. Lettere 1938-1963", in *Giorgio Morandi Roberto Longhi. Opere Lettere Scritti,* cit. 2014, doc. 4, pp. 53-54.

22 "V. inc." followed by a number refers to the general catalogue of prints and its numbering: L. Vitali, *Giorgio Morandi. Opera grafica,* Einaudi Turin, 1957 (2nd revised and expanded ed., 1964; 3rd revised and expanded ed., 1978; 4th expanded ed., 1989).

23 G. Morandi to Roberto Longhi, AFRL, *Corrispondenza, Fascicolo Morandi,* doc. 30, p. 64.

24 R. Longhi, "Avvertenze per il lettore", in *Scritti giovanili 1921-1922 (Opere complete, I, 1),* Sansoni, Florence, 1961, pp. X-XI; and in *Giorgio Morandi Roberto Longhi. Opere Lettere Scritti,* cit. 2014, p. 171.

25 G. Morandi to R. Longhi, 12 November 1961, published in *Giorgio Morandi – Roberto Longhi. Opere Lettere Scritti, cit. 2014, doc. 53, p. 73.*

26 R. Longhi, *Piero della Francesca,* Rome, *Valori Plastici* Edition, 1927.

27 N. Rowley, "A 'Light without Color': Giorgio Morandi and Piero della Francesca", in *Giorgio Morandi 1890-1964,* cit. 2008-2009, pp. 107-117; M.C. Bandera, "Sotto il segno di Cézanne. Il nodo Longhi – Morandi – Piero della Francesca", in *Piero della Francesca. Indagine su un mito,* exhibition catalogue (Forlì, Musei San Domenico, 13 February – 26 June 2016), ed. by A. Paolucci, D. Benati, F. Dabell, F. Mazzocca, P. Refice, and U. Tramonti, Silvana Editoriale, Cinisello Balsamo (Milan), 2016, pp. 331-332.

28 M. C. Bandera, "Giorgio Morandi: la ricerca dell'essenza", in *Giorgio Morandi 1890-1964,* exhibition catalogue (Rome, Complesso del Vittoriano, 28 February – 21 June 2015), ed. by M. C. Bandera, Skira, Milan, 2015, pp. 44-45.

29 R. Longhi, "Giorgio Morandi", preface to the *Mostra Personale di Giorgio Morandi,* in *Catalogo della XXXIII Biennale Internazionale d'Arte,* Venice 1966, p. 22, now in idem, Scritti sull'Otto e Novecento, cit. 1984, p. 93.

30 The list of works only appears in the little catalogue of the Fiore gallery, R. Longhi, *Giorgio Morandi,* cit. 1945, unpaginated.

31 M. C. Bandera, "Morandi non sarà secondo a nessuno", cit. 2014, p. 16.

32 On this painting, listed in a manuscript note as still in Longhi's collection in 1964, see

M.C. Bandera, "The Morandis in the Merlini collection", in *eadem, Giorgio Morandi – Roberto Longhi. Opere Lettere Scritti,* cit. 2014, pp. 161-162.

33 M. Gregori, "Longhi tra antico e moderno", in *Da Renoir a De Staël. Roberto Longhi e il moderno,* exhibition catalogue (Ravenna, Loggetta Lombardesca 23 February – 30 June 2003), ed. by C. Spadoni, Mazzotta, Milan, 2003, p. 16.

34 R. Longhi, *Giorgio Morandi (1945),* cit. 1984, p. 95.

35 R. Longhi, *Giorgio Morandi (1945),* cit. 1984, p. 96.

36 Speaking to Francesca Pini in an interview emblematically entitled "Voglio che la mia Cina s'innamori di Morandi" ("I want China to fall in love with Morandi", in *Sette – Corriere della Sera,* 12, 21 March 2014), the Chinese painter Zeng Fanzhi declared why for loving Morandi led him to collect his work: "When you see a painting and you don't have the words to express the sensations it prompts in you, you are in a state of grace, and if we think that it is the artist who creates beauty, this touches the miraculous. In Morandi we find all these elements, in his small-scale pictures, and his white, pink and grey tonalities contain a sense of the infinite. And to love these works of his there is no need for commentary to decipher what he seeks to express: they all have a marvellous naturalness, they're not inflated, exaggerated, pretentious. And above all they're accessible to every beholder."

37 A. Vettese, "Morandi e la cultura artistica del secondo dopo guerra", in *Morandi ultimo. Nature morte 1950-1964,* exhibition catalogue (Verona, Galleria dello Scudo, 14 December 1997 – 28 February 1998; Venice, Peggy Guggenheim Collection, 30 April – 13 September 1998) ed. by L. Mattioli Rossi, Milan, 1997, pp. 59-68; P. Coldwell, *Morandi's Legacy. Influences in British Art,* exhibition catalogue (Kendall, Abbott Hall, 12 January – 25 March 2006; London, Estorick Collection of Modern Italian Art, 5 April – 18 June 2006), London, 2006; M. Franciolli, "Assonanze", in *Giorgio Morandi,* exhibition catalogue (Lugano, Museo d'Arte Città di Lugano, 10 March – 1 July 2012), ed. by M. C. Bandera and M. Franciolli, Silvana Editoriale, Cinisello Balsamo (Milan), 2012, pp. 200-213; M. Maiorino, *1964-2018: Morandi dopo Morandi,* in *Il dispositivo Morandi. Arte e critica 1934-2018, intr.* by S. Zuliani, Quodlibet, Macerata, 2019, pp. 109-194.

38 See our summary in the recent one-man show: M. C. Bandera, "Giorgio Morandi: Modern Restlessness," in *Giorgio Morandi. A retrospective,* exhibition catalogue (Brussels, Bozar – Palais des Beaux-Arts, 6 June – 22 September 2013), Silvana Editoriale, Cinisello Balsamo (Milan), 2013, pp. 40-41, p. 43 notes 87-98. For a review of the exhibition see B. Schwabsky, "Giorgio Morandi. Center for Fine Arts, Brussels", Artforum, October 2013, pp. 290-291.

39 Tacita Dean, *Still Life (2009), and Day for Night (2009), Fondazione Nicola Trussardi:* these films were initially screened as part of the exhibition in Milan, Palazzo Dugnani, 12 May – 21 June 2009, and on several later occasions. The citation is from the accompanying booklet, p. 23.

40 Tony Cragg in *Morandi's Legacy,* cit. 2006, p. 9.

41 H. Becher interviewed by G. Maraniello, in *Bernd & Hilla Becher at Museo Morandi,* exhibition catalogue (Bologna, Museo Morandi, 24 January – 19 April 2009), ed. by G. Maraniello, Verona 2009, pp. 6-7.

42 L. Carroll, "Palace of Emotions", in *Giorgio Morandi,* cit. 2012, p. 249.

43 L. Carroll, "Palace of Emotions", in *Giorgio Morandi,* cit. 2012, p. 253.

44 *Rachel Whiteread. Study for Room,* exhibition (Bologna, MAMbo – Museo d'Arte Moderna di Bologna, 24 January – 4 May 2014) curated by G. Maraniello, Bologna, 2014.

45 P. P. Pasolini, text from *Irene Brin e Gaspero Del Corso le Annunciano l'inaugurazione della mostra di Renzo Vespignani,* Galleria L'Obelisco, Via Sistina, Rome, 16 November 1956, cited in *M. C. Bandera, Contemporaneità di Morandi,* in *Giorgio Morandi,* cit. 2012, pp. 15 and 16.

46 D. DeLillo, *Falling Man,* New York, 2007, p. 14; Italian ed., *L'uomo che cade,* Einaudi, Turin, 2008, p. 14.

47 P. Auster, *Sunset Park,* New York, 2010, p. 115; Italian ed., *Sunset Park,* Einaudi, Turin, 2010, p. 86, cited by M. C. Bandera, "Contemporaneità di Morandi", in *Giorgio Morandi, cit. 2012,* p. 15.

48 S. Hustvedt, "The drama of perception: Looking at Morandi", in *Giorgio Morandi,* cit. 2012, pp. 254-269.

49 The transcript of the *Interview with Bernardo Bertolucci,* filmed in Rome on 2 February 2012, was published in Giorgio Morandi, cit. 2012, p. 271.

Giorgio Morandi. *Paesaggio*, 1940,
V. 277, oil on canvas, 34.5 × 31 cm (detail)
Courtesy Fondazione di Studi
di Storia dell'Arte Roberto Longhi, Firenze

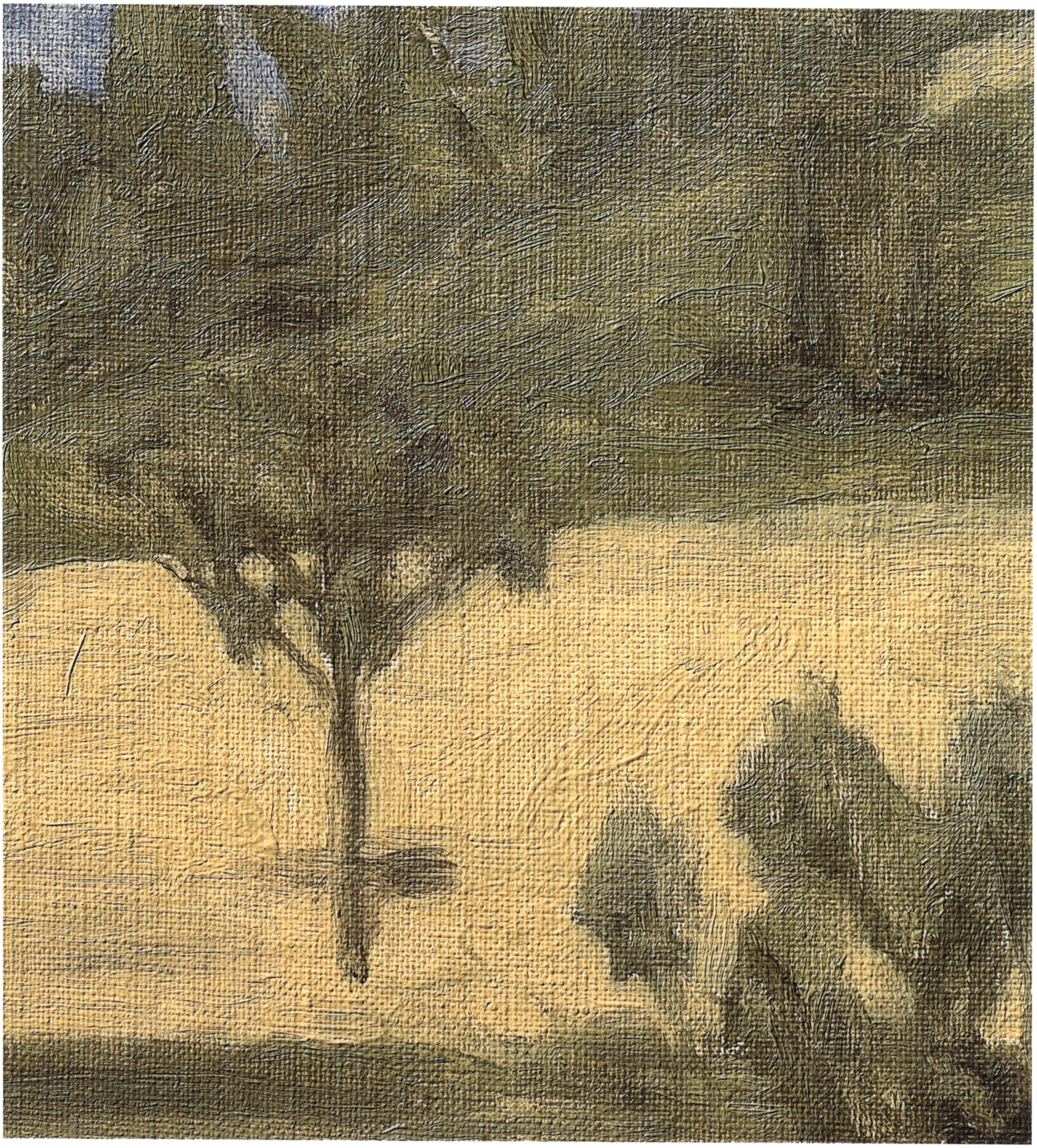

Morandi, another reading

Maria Cristina Bandera

Given the presence in our Florentine exhibition of works by Morandi originally owned by two outstanding art historians, it is worth at least taking brief notice – and deferring further study to a later date – of the painter's rapport with these two individuals, who were a generation younger than him and gave him their critical support, but who above all had the distinct honour of his discerning friendship: the Sienese Cesare Brandi (1906-1988) and the Lucchese Carlo Ludovico Ragghianti (1910-1987). The latter had the added merit of having steered to Florence the collection of early twentieth-century Italian art owned by the Genoese marine engineer Alberto Della Ragione; this was donated to the city in 1970 through Ragghianti's "diligent and magnanimous intervention".[1] This followed the appeal,[2] launched a few months after the flood that inundated Florence in 1966, to set up a museum of contemporary art, which has now taken shape in today's Museo Novecento, the venue for our exhibition. The four works from the Della Ragione collection represent the core of this show: a very rare watercolour, the *Bagnante* [Bather] of 1918[3] (rare because the sheet bears an early date, 11 April 1918, and because of the figure); the *Natura morta* [Still Life], 1923-1924, V. 114; the *Paesaggio* [Landscape], 1936, V. 213; and the *Natura morta* [Still Life], 1938, V. 232.

A significant gesture on Morandi's behalf was made by Cesare Brandi[4], who owned the *Paesaggio* [Landscape], 1934, V. 181 and the *Natura morta* [Still Life], 1957, V. 1057 (which as part of his property, left to the nation,[5] passed into state ownership and is now in the collection of the Pinacoteca di Siena) and the drawings *Natura morta* [Still Life], 1932 and *Fiori* [Flowers], 1939[6] (now Collezione Nazionale d'Arte Moderna e Contemporanea, Rome) which has lent it to the present exhibition. This followed the polemics prompted by his failure to gain the first prize for his monographic show within the *Terza Quadriennale di Roma* of 1939.[7] In support of the painter, the Sienese critic published the article (emblematic in its very title), "Cammino di Morandi", in *Le Arti*, in 1939. The article was the prelude, together with a postscript, of a separate, independent volume of the same title which took on the complete, structured form of an important monograph two years later, in 1941, and was subsequently republished several times.[8]

From that moment on, proving his great and enduring interest for Morandi, Brandi showed his support for the artist through a variety of far-reaching and constant critical responses, compiled in a single volume, *Morandi lungo il cammino*, published in 1970.[9]

For his part, the painter considered the critic a highly-favoured correspondent[10] and one of his most important spokesmen, so much so that he asked him to speak on his behalf on 8 December 1957, in Rome (where Brandi lived when he was director of the Istituto Centrale del Restauro), after winning the international Grand Prize for painting at the São Paulo Biennale;[11] the event was held in the Brazilian Embassy in Palazzo Pamphilj. It was in this speech, *Per conto di Morandi*, and at his explicit request, that Brandi summarised his critical thoughts about the artist, using the occasion to emphasise his "supra-national and universal" role: "whatever the future holds [...] for the fate of painting, and whatever position Italy may still hold in it, it remains a fact that in the international recognition given to Morandi, forty years of Italian painting have gone beyond a national frontier to enter the universal consciousness of our time. And since this is the best form of internationalism, in the recognition of the universality and perennially contemporary quality of its form, this is why the prize awarded to Morandi assumes for us a significance greater than the prize itself." [12]

Giorgio Morandi and Carlo Ludovico Ragghianti had met in the Palazzo delle Esposizio-

Carlo Ludovico Ragghianti. Courtesy Fondazione Licia e Carlo Ludovico Ragghianti, Fototeca Carlo Ludovico Ragghianti, Lucca

ni during the *Seconda Quadriennale* of 1935 in Rome, as the latter was to recall in the Florentine daily newspaper *La Nazione*,[13] but it was in Bologna, five years later, that they began to see each other frequently, when the art historian was there in mandatory residence because of his anti-Fascist militancy: "From 1940 onwards Morandi, whom I had met in 1935, was a friend of mine and of my wife, initially in Bologna, where we lived for some time. Almost every day he would come up to us to chat and listen to Radio Londra".[14] As we know, it was precisely because of this association that Morandi was arrested in April 1943 and incarcerated in the San Giovanni in Monte jail. He was released on 30 May after Roberto Longhi had interceded on his behalf with Giuseppe Bottai, who was then the Minister of National Education. To interweave the histories of our characters here, we may note that in 1914 Bottai had been Longhi's pupil at the Liceo Tasso in Rome, together with Lucia Lopresti (later known as Anna Banti), who became Longhi's wife. As a sign of his gratitude Morandi presented the Longhis with the small canvas of *Fiori* [Flowers], 1943, V. 408,[15] one of the outstanding pictures in the present exhibition.

Although this cultural and human friendship[16] was not interrupted by Ragghianti's return to Florence (indeed the two men continued to correspond regularly[17]), his first important essay on the painter did not appear until 1954.[18] This was republished in 1982, together with other extensive texts that contain the critic's views on Morandi, in a volume entitled *Bologna cruciale 1914*.[19] It is striking how Ragghianti's interpretative acuity was the first to focus (and immediately so) on "the architectural substance of Morandi's art" by making an unusual but eloquent juxtaposition with one of the great architects of organic architecture, Frank Lloyd Wright – himself the object for the first time of a major exhibition in Italy, held in the Palazzo Strozzi in Florence and curated by Oscar Stonorov, with the collaboration of Ragghianti.[20]

"I would say", wrote the latter, "with an evident paradox, that only someone with the ability (or strength) to understand Wright can understand Morandi in how he truly creates".[21] This conviction led him to state that Morandi "draws, and tests the plans of his compositions, and thus also calculates how planes and volumes fill the space; he tries out the distances, opens out or brings forward the backgrounds, the sides, and the top and bottom with respect to the dimensions; he balances the range and correlation of the bodies, and launches the network of shadows and lights". Ragghianti then concludes that looking at his 'still lifes' one should speak of "cathedrals rather than bottles".[22]

This was a very sharp-minded critical reading, not only because it helps us to get beyond the "common tale of the painter of bottles"[23] and understand how Morandi's 'bottles' are not the 'reproduction' of everyday objects but rather elementary forms of different height and proportion, useful for articulating a composition along its vertical axis (and for this reason rendered 'neutral' by the pigment or white gesso applied to them, thus depriving them of their transparency and mimetic value), but also because it was far-sighted. Distant in time and space – in the new millennium and overseas – a concrete visual presence emerged in the juxtaposition made by the American film director Sydney Pollack, in his documentary *Sketches of Frank Gehry*, between the eight small geometrical bodies in the *Still Life*, 1956, V. 985 (Bologna, Museo Morandi; but the image is reversed in the film) and the forms and volumes of the Winton Guest House by the celebrated Canadian architect.[24]

A result of Ragghianti's constant attention to how Morandi worked is also reflected in the

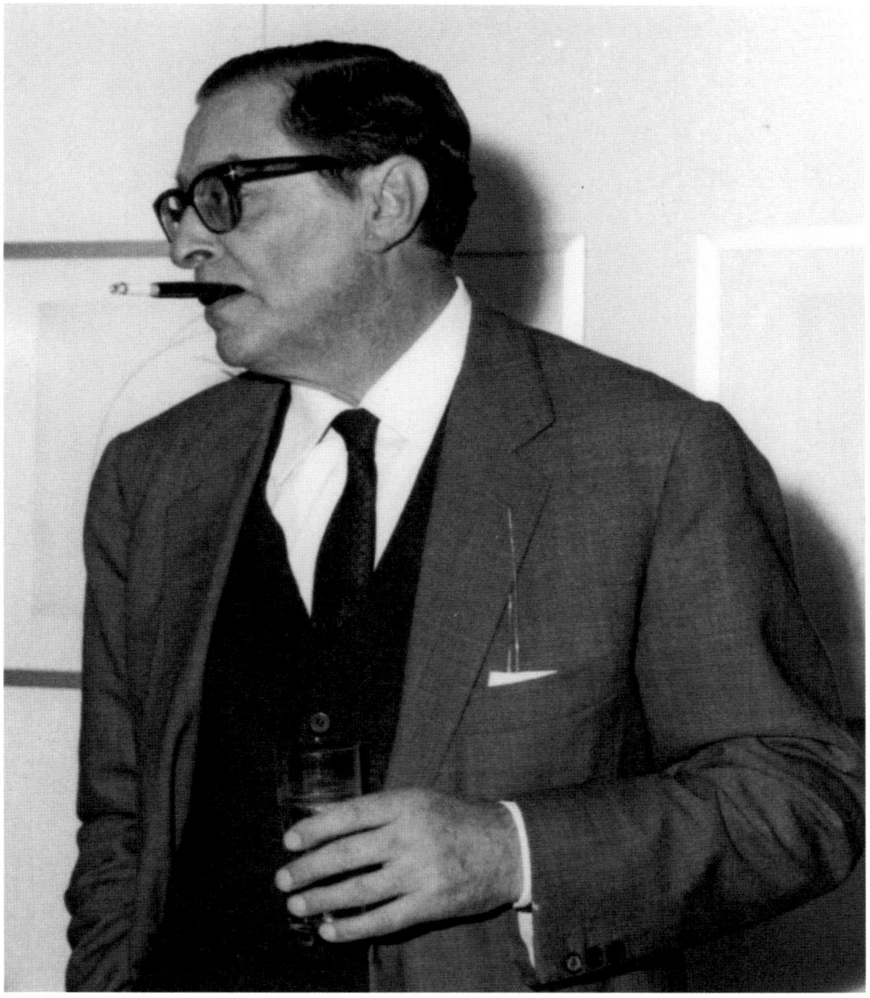

ultimate destiny of the *Natura morta* [Still Life] of 1942,[25] given to him by the painter – another piece of invaluable documentation exhibited here. Its story is related by the art historian in the caption next to the illustration in his book, whose title, *Arte, fare, vedere*, emphasises his attention to the creative process: "in conversation with Ragghianti, Morandi expressed his concern that the objects were thinning out in the upper part, and before his speechless interlocutor he unnailed the canvas, grabbed a large pair of tailor's scissors and swiftly cut it along the top (with such lucidity of thought, in its undulation, with respect to the forms). Having looked at it at arm's length for a little while, he spoke briefly: 'Now it's better', and offering me the rolled-up canvas, he added: 'You hold on to it'."[26]

This is a work before which today's public, to which we all belong, can only ask themselves this: what did it look like initially? What did that 'cut' mean? What did Morandi mean by "it's better"? And, above all, what thoughts were crossing that creative mind of his?

1 See *La raccolta Alberto Della Ragione, Museo d'Arte Contemporanea di Firenze*, Cassa di Risparmio di Firenze, Florence, 1970 (including "Un ricordo e un omaggio di Ragghianti", pp. XV-XVIII); and F. Scalia, ed., *Raccolta d'Arte Contemporanea Alberto Della Ragione*, Florence, 1987.

2 Ragghianti made his appeal during *Arte moderna in Italia 1915-1935*, the exhibition he personally curated (Florence, Palazzo Strozzi, 26 February-28 May 1967).

3 The general catalogue reference is P. 1918/1: M. Pasquali, *Morandi. Acquerelli. Catalogo generale,* Electa, Milan, 1991.

4 For Brandi and Morandi's friendship, see M. I. Catalano, *Lungo il cammino. Cesare Brandi 1933-1943*, Siena 2007, *passim*; *Cesare Brandi Morandi, con il carteggio Brandi-Morandi*, ed. by M. Pasquali, Protagon Editori Toscani, Siena, 2008, *passim* (and especially therein, *eadem*, "Diciotto anni dopo", pp. 17-28, and V. Brandi Rubiu, "Brandi, Morandi, l'estetica e altre cose", pp. 177-180).

5 A. M. Guiducci, "La villa di Cesare Brandi a Vignano: una donazione allo Stato", in *La passione e l'arte. Cesare Brandi e Luigi Magnani collezionisti*, exhibition catalogue (Siena, Complesso Museale di Santa Maria della Scala – Palazzo Squarcialupi, 8 December 2006-11 March 2007), edited by L. Fornari Schianchi and A. M. Guiducci, Umberto Allemandi, Turin, 2006, pp. 23-29.

6 The general catalogue references are T.P. 1932/7 e T.P. 1939/1: E. Tavoni, M. Pasquali, *Morandi. Disegni. Catalogo generale,* Electa, Milano, 1994.

7 On that occasion the prize was awarded to Bruno Saetti.

8 C. Brandi, "Cammino di Morandi", *Le Arti*, 1939, reprinted, together with the *Poscritto*, 1941, most recently in *idem*, *Scritti d'arte*, edited by V. Rubiu Brandi, Milan, 2013, pp. 623-659.

9 C. Brandi, *Morandi lungo il cammino*, Rizzoli, Milan 1970; most recently reprinted in *idem*, *Morandi lungo il cammino*, edited by V. Brandi Rubiu, Castelvecchi, Rome 2014.

10 M. Pasquali, "Carteggio Brandi-Morandi 1936-1964", in *Cesare Brandi Morandi*, cit. 2008, pp. 191-350.

11 For the events leading to the prize awarded at the Biennale in São Paulo in 1957, see M. C. Bandera,

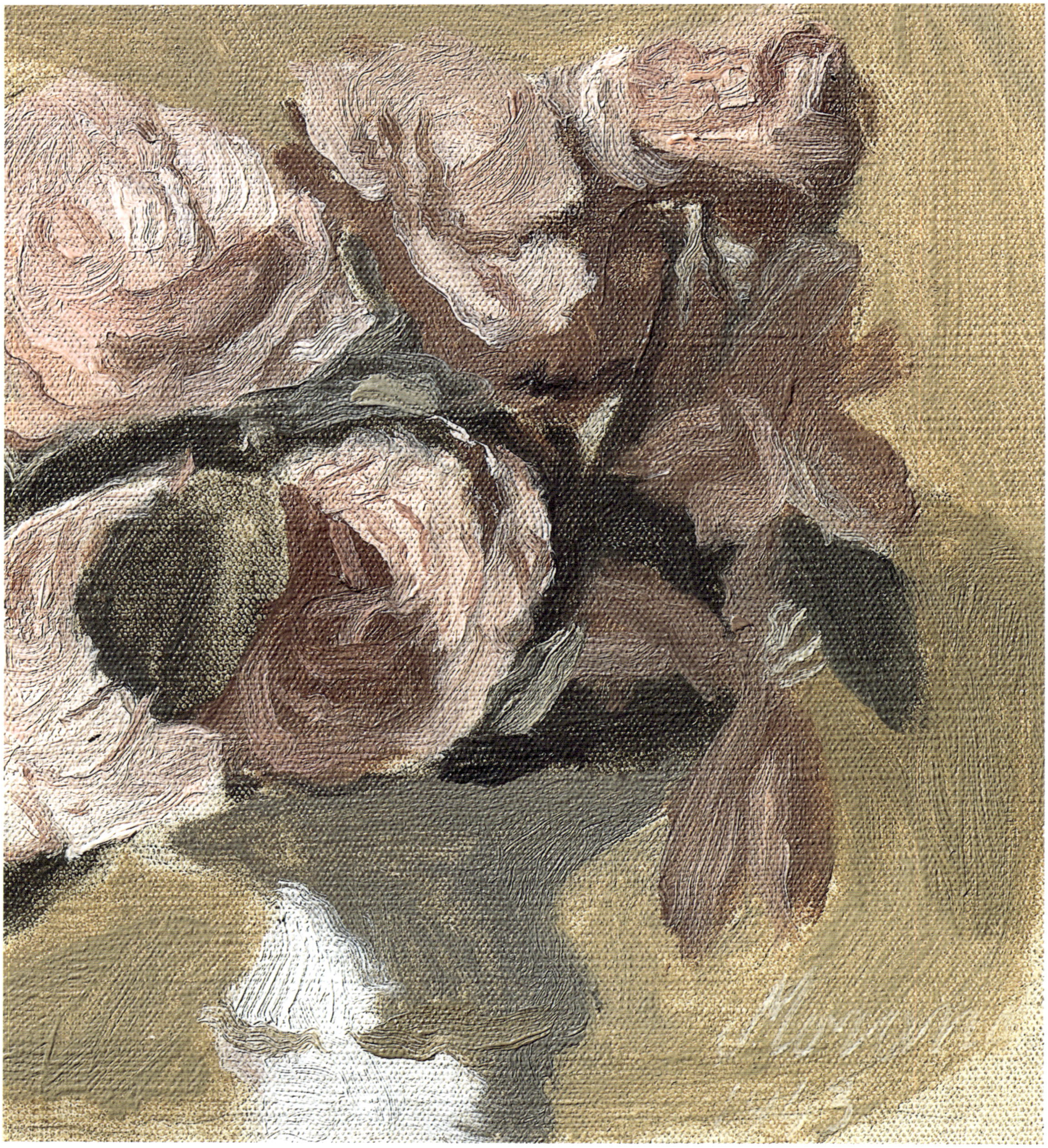

Giorgio Morandi. *Fiori*, 1943,
V. 408, oil on canvas, 20.7 × 25.3 cm (detail)
Courtesy Fondazione di Studi di Storia
dell'Arte Roberto Longhi, Firenze

"Prefazione", in *Morandi sceglie Morandi. Corrispondenza con la Biennale 1947-1962*, Charta, Milan, 2001, *passim*, and specifically pp. 24-43.

12 C. Brandi, *Per conto di Morandi* (1957), now in *idem*, *Morandi lungo il cammino*, cit. 2014, p. 92.

13 C. L. Ragghianti, "Geometria di Morandi", in *La Nazione*, Tuesday 8 April 1985, p. 3. This was a review of *Fiori di Giorgio Morandi*, with texts by G. Testori and J. M. Folon, Geneva and Milan 1985, reprinted in *idem*, "Piante di Morandi", *Critica d'Arte*, 4th series, LI, 10, July-September 1986, pp. 23-24.

14 *Ibid.*

15 See the letter Morandi wrote to Longhi from Bologna on 12 March 1954, published by M. C. Bandera, in *Giorgio Morandi-Roberto Longhi. Lettere 1938-1963*, in *Giorgio Morandi Roberto Longhi. Opere Lettere Scritti*, cit. 2014, p. 66, doc. 37. The artist asked whether Longhi might lend the canvas of "roses without a vase that I painted after I was freed from San Giovanni in Monte" to the forthcoming exhibition at The Hague.

16 On the intellectual friendship between Morandi and Ragghianti see M. C. Bandera, in *Morandi e Firenze. I suoi amici critici e collezionisti*, exhibition catalogue (Florence, Fondazione di Studi di Storia dell'Arte Roberto Longhi, 21 January–6 March 2005) ed. by M. C. Bandera, Mazzotta, Milan, 2005, pp. 27-33; and *Tre voci. Carlo L. Ragghianti, Cesare Gnudi, Giorgio Morandi*, ed. by M. Pasquali and S. Bulgarelli, Gli Ori, Pistoia 2010.

17 *Carteggio tra Carlo Ludovico Ragghianti e Giorgio Morandi 1943-1964*, ed. by M. Pasquali, in *Tre voci. Carlo L. Ragghianti Cesare Gnudi Giorgio Morandi*, cit. 2010, pp. 107-135.

18 C. L. Ragghianti, "Giorgio Morandi", *La Critica d'Arte*, I, January 1954, p. 50. This is a reprint of his text in the exhibition catalogue of the collection of Gianni Mattioli, *Arte moderna in una raccolta italiana* (Florence, La Strozzina, April-May 1953), Edizioni del Milione, Milan, 1953, pp. 12-17. See also Ragghianti's fundamental essay "Morandi o l'architettura della visione", in *idem*, *Bologna cruciale 1914 e saggi su Morandi, Gorni, Saetti*, Bologna (*Opere di C. L. Ragghianti*, VIII) 1982, pp. 221-253.

19 C. L. Ragghianti, *Bologna cruciale 1914*, cit. 1982.

20 *Mostra di Frank Lloyd Wright* (Florence, Palazzo Strozzi, April-June 1951), curated by O. Stonorov with the assistance of C. L. Ragghianti.

21 C. L. Ragghianti, "Giorgio Morandi", 1954, now "Morandi interiore", in *Bologna cruciale 1914*, cit. 1982, p. 196.

22 C. L. Ragghianti, "Giorgio Morandi", 1954, now "Morandi interiore", in *Bologna cruciale 1914*, cit. 1982, p. 201.

23 F. Arcangeli, *Giorgio Morandi*, Edizioni del Milione, Milan, 1964, p. 280.

24 S. Pollack, *Sketches of Frank Gehry*, USA: Sony Pictures Classics, 2006.

25 M. Pasquali, *Morandi. Opere catalogate tra il 1985 e il 2000*, Museo Morandi – Musica Insieme, Bologna, 2000.

26 C. L. Ragghianti, *Arte, fare e vedere dall'arte al museo*, Vallecchi, Florence, 1974, p. 111.

Giorgio Morandi
Elévage de Poussière

Claudio Parmiggiani

His house reminded me a lot of my aunt Onorina's in Suzzara.
Windows half closed to keep out the world.
Everything was still, apart from the tick-tock of a pendulum.
Around it, a wall clock on which the dusty glass rendered the hours opaque.
On a shelf, a candlestick.
Against the wall, hanging from a nail, a thermometer and a mirror.
Enclosed by a frame, a fragment of illuminated parchment.
Here and there, small shelves arranged like mini-theatres held jars,
bottles, cups, jugs, vials, lamps.
Hour glasses; filters of a celestial pharmacy.
Encrusted with coagulated paints accumulated over time, a three-legged easel,
almost an instrument for a very slow martyrdom.
Rags impregnated with paint.
Paint brushes everywhere.
A small Noah's Ark containing the more philosophical things;
the silent, humble object of the everyday gaze.
The house of a child.
Gathered inside, things consisting of everything and nothing.
He did not conceive different subjects but an image.
An image for ever.
To dwell on a face for a lifetime and a lifetime means that the face dwells on us.
Inside a vial, the universe.
A monk, a lamp, his philosophical desert.
In his studio it was possible to understand the metaphysical meaning of dust.
I often went to see him in via Fondazza on summer afternoons,
and in the half-light of the kitchen he talked about Piero and the Carraccis.
To protect his eyes from the light he would often lift a hand to his forehead,
like someone peering at the horizon.
On my first visit to see Morandi
I was accompanied by Father Gianni Poggeschi,
a gentle shadow.
One afternoon in June 1959.

Giorgio Morandi. *Paesaggio*, 1941,
V. 342, oil on canvas, 41.5 × 52.7 cm (detail)
Courtesy Private Collection, Firenze

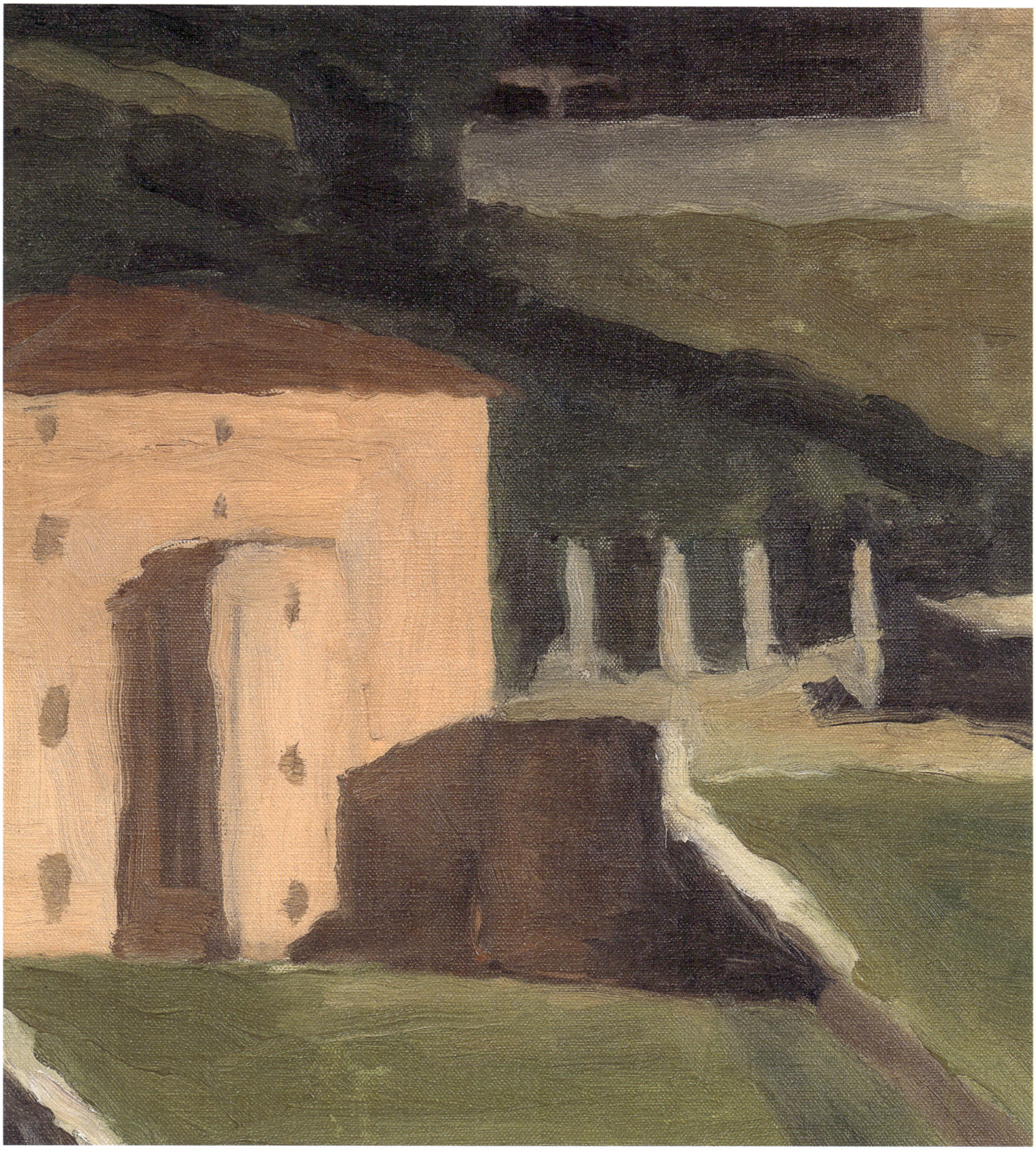

Giorgio Morandi: Resistance and Persistence

Sean Scully

Giorgio Morandi was born in Bologna in 1890. He studied art at the Accademia di Belle Arti from 1907-15.

He lived all his life with his three sisters, Anna, Dina and Maria Teresa. From the age of 20 until his death he lived in a flat at Via Fordazza 36, and in the family country house in Grizzana in the mountains 35 km from Bologna. He traveled to Venice where he saw Monet and Cézanne, but largely throughout his life he moved very little, being content to live and work in his simple rooms in Bologna, and his home in Grizzana. And it was only in 1956, at the age of 66, that Morandi made his one and only trip abroad, which was to attend an opening of an exhibition he had in Winterthur. Morandi died in Bologna in 1964.

Crucially, Morandi never visited Paris, the center of Art in the first half of the 20th century, which is like not visiting New York or London now. When I was a student passing through the halls of the Tate Gallery in London, looking for role models, I would consistently pass a typically small painting by Morandi. It seemed to upset and disturb everything else that was going on. It was as if it was participating in the modernist dialogue, since its spirit was 20th century, and clearly painted after the discovery of Abstraction, but then again, stubbornly refusing to participate with appropriate enthusiasm. It seemed to be permanently hung on a short wall. So you saw it between seeing other paintings that were of course always bigger. Everything, it seemed, was bigger than the Morandi. Nothing else was as self-effacing. And nothing else was so awkwardly sealed. So you'd see Morandi after you'd looked at one painting and you turned your body and your head to look at the next, and as you were leaving one room to go into another room you'd see the Morandi again. Not fitting in. NOT playing the game. Being a part of it and not being a part of it, so therefore in the margin of the communal conversation, the common consensus built by the surrounding works. Imagine one sees, for example, a short wall, between big walls that occupy major spaces, as the margin of the architecture, or the transition between one major event and the next; this is where Morandi lived in the museum. Not exactly an event but a tap on the back of the head. An appeal to the conscience one might say. A worrying doubt. Made by a doubter: who raises the disturbing possibility that the modernist juggernaut that we were so happy about, might one day crash and burn.

And then there would be this small painting that says, "yes". This kind of thing can happen. And it has happened before. Rome was for 4000 years the center of the universe known to man. And it is therefore very Italian to know that the favors of history can wash in and then wash out leaving empty buildings and unfortunately located agendas.

One day I'd see it and I'd think, this is great. It's really weird. And then another day I'd see it and I'd think to myself that he was an idiot. And so was the Tate for putting it up all the time. And then another day I'd see it and I just didn't know what to think. It wasn't exciting yet it was exciting. Exciting in its resistance, in its subversiveness. Someone asked me once if Abstraction was subversive. I did not think so. And I don't think so now. It's subversive in the sense that it makes or helps people to think free. But it's not trying to bring some other structure down to be seen. It makes it's own space or has invented its own space. A space, that didn't previously exist. This, coincidentally, Morandi did. This small painting used a space that was not used before, or could not usefully be used by anything else. The architecture of the idea, was to say yes. Correct. But what about this? That was big, this is small. That was a statement, this is a state.

Giorgio Morandi. *Natura morta*, 1937 ca.-1938 ca., V. 232, oil on canvas, 42 x 63 cm (detail)
Courtesy Collezioni Civiche, Raccolta Alberto Della Ragione, Firenze

That Morandi was making an art of figuration during an epoch characterized by a wholesale march towards Abstraction was, in itself, an act of defiance. However in his case the defiance was wrapped in a cloak made of humble subversion. His paintings were not merely opposite in subject. His "opposite" subject was painted apparently meekly in colors that were pale and seemingly tired, as if defeated at the outset of their contest with international Abstraction. Like a boxer who fights each round without getting up from his seat in the corner of the ring. As if in a sense to make a demonstration of rising for the contest, would be far too conformist and compromising. Morandi paints in pale, nearly dead color, which itself cannot or will not rise to full spectrum. It will not reach across space to communicate visual power, but makes you reach across space toward it. We do the walking. The painting does the waiting. It lets you, in fact invites you to walk past it and ignore it: It is only after you have seen many other paintings that you return to it, with your doubt. Morandi embodies the patience and the diffidence of history.

The undersized painting that is pallid at birth, doesn't need to be defeated by time and by its offspring history. Morandi, who is full of history, understands it can begin in life that way. As if it has already been weakened by time as it is being made.

Morandi, the priest of subversion and reverence, sits in his small room stroking his humble surfaces with a vibrating acceptance of the impossibilities and necessity of resistance. Resistance to the majority and resistance to progress. When Fascism was rising in Europe like a galloping fire, Giorgio Morandi was a young man at art school, and trying to articulate his place in the contemporary world.

He began his public life as an artist with an active dialogue with the visual ideas of his day, the most dominant of which was Cubism. His landscape and still life paintings from around 1913 and 1914 demonstrate a willingness to do what all young artists must do: which is to learn the lessons of recent Art. However in Morandi's case this dialogue is short lived, and his rejection of Internationalism is born of a deeply felt negative reaction to war and its consequences. Thus Morandi began his unique journey by traveling in the opposite direction to his contemporaries.

The Act of Looking with Cézanne

To see and to work. To paint in a way that was predetermined and to paint a subject that was always virtually the same. Thus to simultaneously liberate the painting style which represented the subject without prejudice: as I would call it, and the freedom to read that subject as space, light, color and form. Morandi paints things that exist, though they are stripped of all burdensome references to social function and history or political contexts. His discreetly expressive painting style is in concert with a subject that is also discreet, in the sense that they are vessels and containers who's meaning is open and exists outside clear political or functional reference. We are free to enjoy them and feel them as we might an abstract painting, yet they are faithful and mysterious representations of objects that were there. Huddled together in familial dependencies. So that their edges touch, and the bodily groupings and their contact enables them to stand humble yet noble on their simple shelf. They stand for themselves, but they don't articulate exactly what that is.

The sameness of his subject amplifies the imaginative response. He has learned the lessons of Abstraction. He has understood how

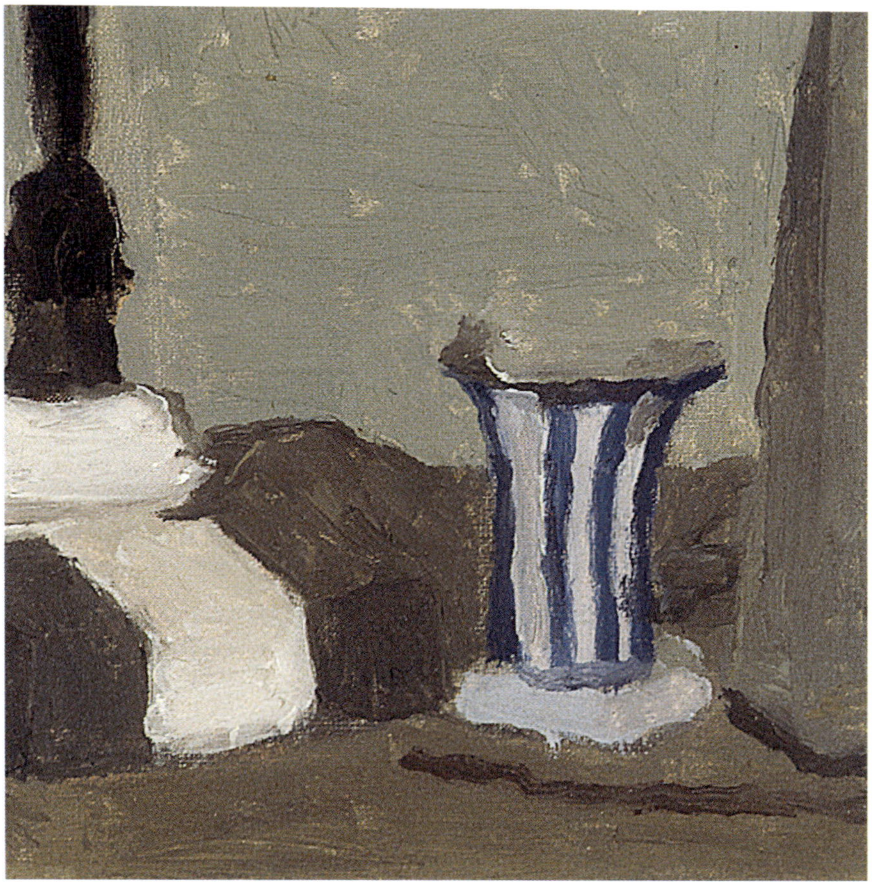

powerfully repetition, and visiting the same or similar motif again and again can open up emotional depth and interpretive range. Abstraction abstracted reality to reach the non-objective shore of new experience. Morandi reverses this journey and returns this possibility to simple observed reality. In this he is very different from Cézanne, his great example. Cézanne never knew Abstraction until he was an old man, even though he pioneered it by making painting systematic. Yet, in his way, he overcame appearance with structure. This, Morandi did not have to do, since the appearances of things in the world had already been conquered by Abstraction.

I once watched a film of Cézanne painting. He moved as a bird moves, and his head was rapidly inclined toward the subject, the canvas, the subject and the canvas. Back and forth in a triangular relationship between the painter, the subject and the painting. This, Morandi did also, since he was painting his jars or the view out of his window in Grizzana. Always in a triangle. When I paint I look at the canvas on the wall, and I paint it. I move back and forth, between my seat and the painting, in a straight line, between me and the work. The painting being the subject and the object, all in one. There is no triangle. Everything I need to make the painting is in me when I start. And this difference is crucial. There are similarities, but the difference is profound.

Robert Irwin has described Morandi as making a unique kind of Abstract Expressionism. While being able to identify with this generous view, and being equally in favor of Morandi's work as Irwin, I would describe Morandi oppositely. The Abstract Expressionists worked in an atmosphere that benefited from group support, and furthermore their position in world culture was advanced from being in the right place at the right time. The various group photographs that were taken of de Kooning, Pollock, Krasner, Motherwell, Newman et al testify to the cultural momentum of which they were the positive recipients. The Abstract Expressionists were working harmoniously with contemporary cultural history and their careers were enlarged accordingly. They were working on the back of European Art, as exemplified by Surrealism and Geometric Abstraction, whilst rejecting and improving it in favor of a new "heroic" American Art. They had the writers such as Greenberg, Sandler and Hess, and the monied patrons such as Peggy Guggenheim, as well as the construction of new Art palaces in America to contextualize critically, to buy and exhibit, these powerful new works.

The simple fact that Morandi, even today, still represents a "cause" that other artists feel obliged to assist, shows how resistable the work of Morandi was. Morandi's paintings were not really collected, because they simply didn't fit. Because when the great collections of America and Europe were being assembled in the fifties and sixties what largely "fitted" was major Abstraction.

Many painters like to argue that the "subject" of Morandi is not important, and that one can ignore the figuration on his work, in order to enjoy the Abstraction. However Morandi's

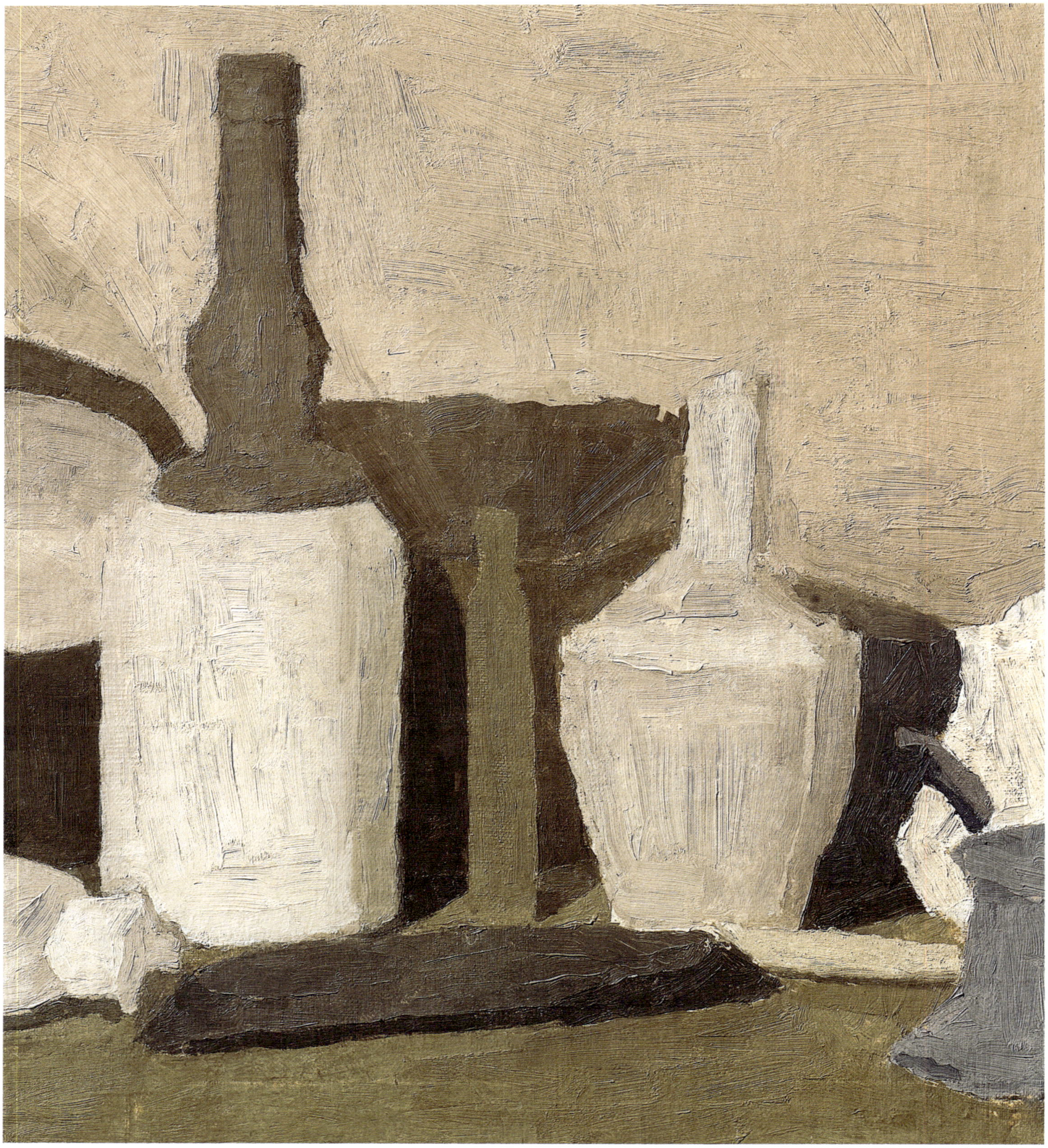

Giorgio Morandi. *Natura morta (natura morta di oggetti in viola)*, 1937, V. 222, oil on canvas, 61.8 × 76.3 cm (detail)
Courtesy Fondazione di Studi di Storia dell'Arte Roberto Longhi, Firenze

work was ignored by the major institutions for good reason. And simply put, it is not Abstract. And it therefore cannot even legitimately be seen as a form of Abstract Expressionism. It should be read as figuratively based.

As a counterweight to the dominance of American painting of the fifties, Morandi holds a position that cannot be challenged, and today seems to yield an array of possible influences and examples for young painters. Morandi's work doesn't negotiate with Abstract Expressionism as does, say, the work of the important French artist, Yves Klein, who competes with America for scale and conceptual directness, or like other Europeans such as Soulages, Schumacher and Tàpies who worked on a similarly large scale. Morandi's extreme originality is achieved as a counter-point to all this. He is the authentic opposite. He doesn't attempt to compete with American Art: he does the contrary, which is what American Art cannot do since no culture can effectively represent the opposite of itself.

I was talking to a friend once on the 'phone about a painting I had just finished. The painting is called *Wall of Light Sky*. She was asking me to describe it. After a few minutes I said, "look, I can describe it to you, by describing something that can't really exist." I told her, since it was made of many greys that were mixed in with pink and red and blue, that it was maybe like a Morandi on a giant scale that was drawn on a broken grid. So I was talking of the way a simple subject could be given a compressed complex history, by being overpainted in uncertain colors. This made everything clear to her even though I had described the impossible: since a giant Morandi is the opposite of what a Morandi is. What its sense of being is, and what it registers itself as in the world of Art.

Morandi is the opposite of heroic-scale Abstraction in every way. That Morandi worked in isolation is part of the central meaning of his work. He chose to resist Modernism in a way that Jackson Pollock did not and did not have to. Pollock, for example, was working in a rising culture that had just won a world war, and played a major role in defeating fascism. The United States had been flooded with grateful, eager to be patriotic immigrants after World War II, and it was glowing with self-belief. New York represented openness and freedom and importantly: wealth. There was no reason why its artists should resist its direction. They were, after all, the equivalent of Masaccio working in Florence in the 14th century. New York was the new Florence, and was a golden gate to a future of freedom and wealth.

Morandi's world was very different. His world was not big, in the sense that it was expanding into light. It was small, in the sense that in the midst of personal crisis, fascism and impending darkness, Morandi had to paint in a corner out of "what was left". What he could salvage. Not what was possible, in terms of invention, growth and freedom: but what he could hold onto, as a human being, in a context of failed hope and danger.

In 1915, when Italy entered World War I, Morandi was conscripted into the Italian army. This event caused him to suffer a nervous breakdown.

It is also the case that politically speaking, Modernism, as exemplified by Futurism in Italy, had been on occasions loosely connected with Fascism. After his breakdown Morandi withdrew into a quiet life of teaching. There he could create a distance from the polarized world of political extremes, war, and the Italian avante garde. This is when, I believe, Morandi began to actively separate himself from the International community of artists, to create his own private space populated by his mute, hand sized, familiar figures. The subject, of his

Giorgio Morandi. *Natura morta*, 1956,
V. 1005, oil on canvas, 4.5 × 4.5 cm (detail)
Courtesy Collezione Banca Monte dei Paschi di Siena

intimate scale vases and boxes and jars, gave him stability and the peace vital for his mental well-being. With this extremely unique subject he was able to rebuild himself emotionally, and begin the gradual formulation of a great understated body of work that was a return to small scale painting in the tradition of Chardin and Manet.

His personal crisis in the face of the non-negotiable image of progress, as widely understood in 1915 Italy, is what forced him to turn away from Modernism. His escape and his solution is what have made him into a great artist for us today. We still revere the modernist masters of the 20th century, though now they seem as if they are from another age. However Morandi sits more comfortably and truthfully for us, on our highway of doubt. His alternative to Modernism corresponds with the temperature of our own time, precisely because it is anti-heroic and therefore the opposite of Abstract Expressionism.

During the years immediately after his breakdown, Morandi was still engaged in a Modernism of sorts: though now it was Pittura Metafisica. In reality this meant he was gradually moving away from Internationalism and the influence of Cubism towards a National style. It is symbolically important that in his Pittura Metafisica period Morandi painted a form of construction or still life that was contained within its own box. Cubism broke up the solidity of the object, fractured it and spread it out over the picture plane. Pittura Metafisica, as exemplified by Morandi's painting, *Natura morta* [Still Life] 1918 (Galleria Nazionale d'Arte Moderna, Rome), established a dream world where objects sit silently and in a protected context. They are secure and framed inside the picture and therefore, metaphorically and symbolically, not in direct contact with the outside world. By 1920 Morandi had positioned himself in his own box, which was his modest studio, where began to paint his "still life" paintings in solitude. This represents a journey away from international engagement, through a National engagement, and ultimately into a private world where he stayed for the rest of his working life.

Modernism represented by the Futurists Boccioni, Severini and Balla stood for progress in the painting world of Italy in 1913. The interaction with the machine and its dynamic movement was reflected powerfully in their paintings. Their engagement with the machine world was responsible for their force since they fed off the juggernaut of progress. However like the Suprematists and Constructivists before them in Russia, the paintings of the Futurists lacked sensibility. One only has to look at the paintings of Rosanova and Malevič to see that they are painted with a kind of generic neutrality. To find a profoundly personal painting style for the Suprematists or the Futurists was not the point of their work or of their mission, which was to represent in paint an International idea. The representation of movement in for example, *Cane al guinzaglio* [Dog on a Leash] 1912 by Giacomo Balla is dynamic, but it is also mechanical in style. This undoubtedly was the point, since an overly subjective or personal worldview would have appeared anti-progressive and bourgeois.

It is against this backdrop of Fascism, Modernism and its opposition to a personal and private sense of poetry that Morandi made his small revolution. This radical resistance, a stand for the individual as a spiritual being, made with humble work in a small room in Bologna should not be underestimated. By slowly withdrawing into his own private box, Morandi constructed a reality that gave him time to think and work against the way large masses of Europe were moving. Morandi worked in the

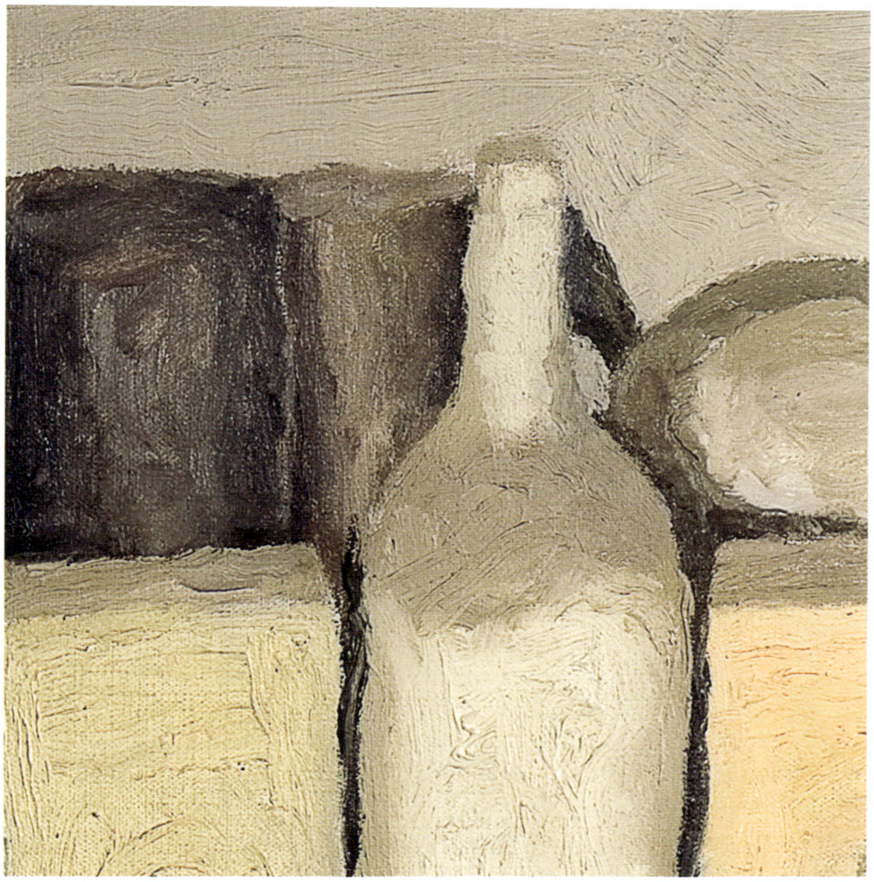

shadows of his studio, for the existential position, to feel as an individual. This is fundamental to the gradual formulation of a masterful sensibility.

Morandi paints like no other, before or since. His brushstroke is in complete philosophical agreement with the subject, the scale and the color of his paintings. It is expressive, though it is modest, and not so expressionistic as to disturb the sense of meditative silence that inhabits all his works.

Still Life c.1957 (The University of Iowa Museum of Art) carries a signature in the left lower corner that is huge in relation to the size of the painting. The signature stands for the individual as author. And for the uniqueness of touch that runs through the painting. As is typical of Morandi the color is pale and profoundly gentle. Two jars, two boxes and one vertical bashful shape, probably standing for a jar, huddles protected in the middle of the group, partially hidden by the bodies of its familial neighborly objects. All the figures close the space between them, and all the figures contain space within their bodies. The absence of earth color gives the two front figures weight and absence of weight simultaneously, so they appear lit-up. The two boxes behind them make a backdrop that has sculptural force. The central figure is compressed, pushed into the position of protected and captive. This quiet drama takes place on a grey, bent interior horizon which gives the centralized composition its place, and its insecurity. Morandi's hand is everywhere, dominating the weak color, yet allowing the whole composition to pulsate evenly. Even the shadows running around the figures as a dark grey collar locks them into place, and the light from the back of the surface is allowed to leak out through the laconic brushstrokes of the painter. He is timeless yet vital, timorous and seemingly threatened by something outside, yet determined and stoic in his will to be. To be human. To stand noble, modest and resistant to the violence of the world.

First published in

S. Scully, *Resistance and Persistence: Selected Writings*, edited by F. Ingleby, Merrell Publishers, London, 2006 and republished in S. Scully, *Inner: The Collected Writings and Selected Interviews of Sean Scully*, Hatje Cantz, Berlin, 2016.

Works

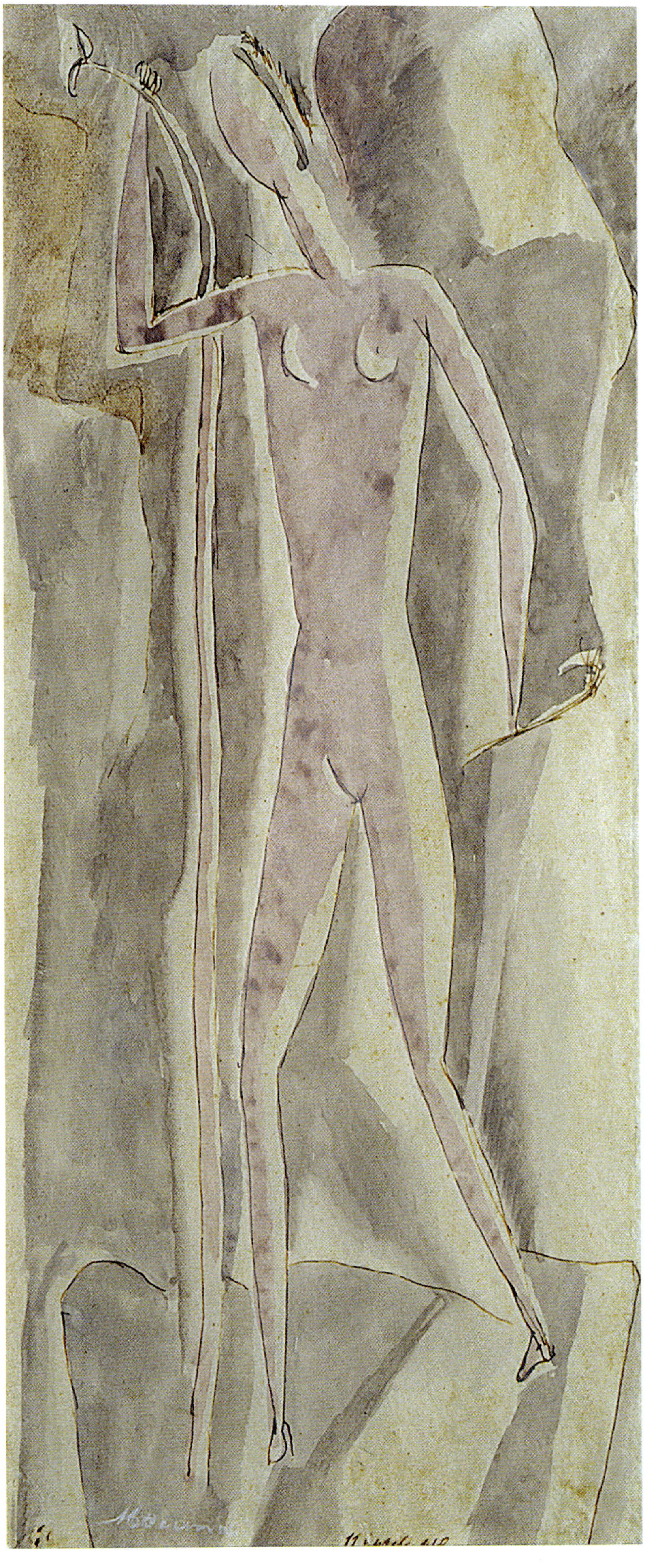

Bagnante, 1918,
P. 1918/1, watercolor on paper, 24 × 10 cm
Courtesy Collezioni Civiche,
Raccolta Alberto Della Ragione, Firenze

Natura morta, 1923-1924,
V. 114, oil on canvas, 60 × 60 cm
Courtesy Collezioni Civiche,
Raccolta Alberto Della Ragione, Firenze

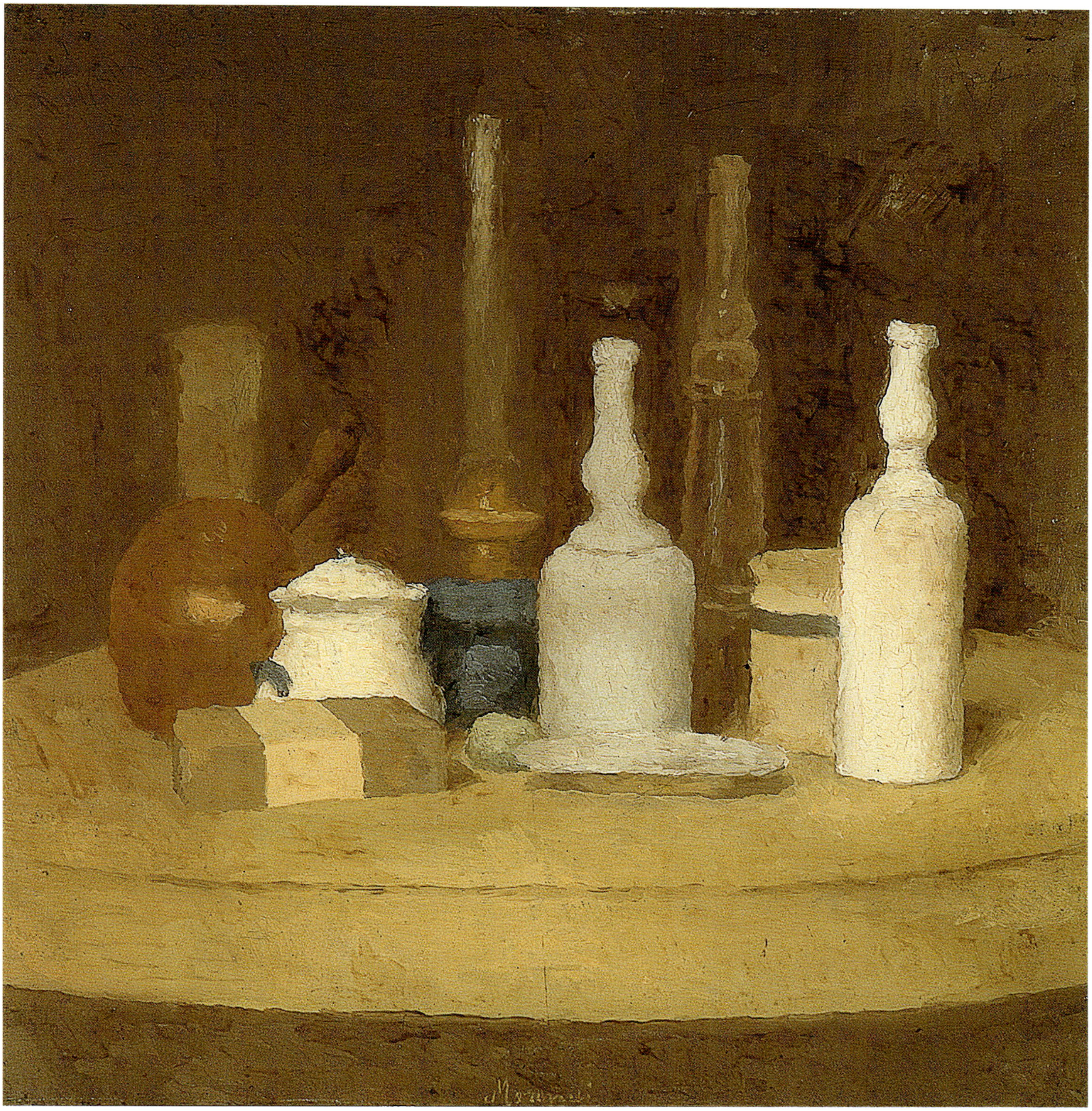

Natura morta, 1929,
V. 151, oil on canvas, 30 × 60 cm
Courtesy Private Collection

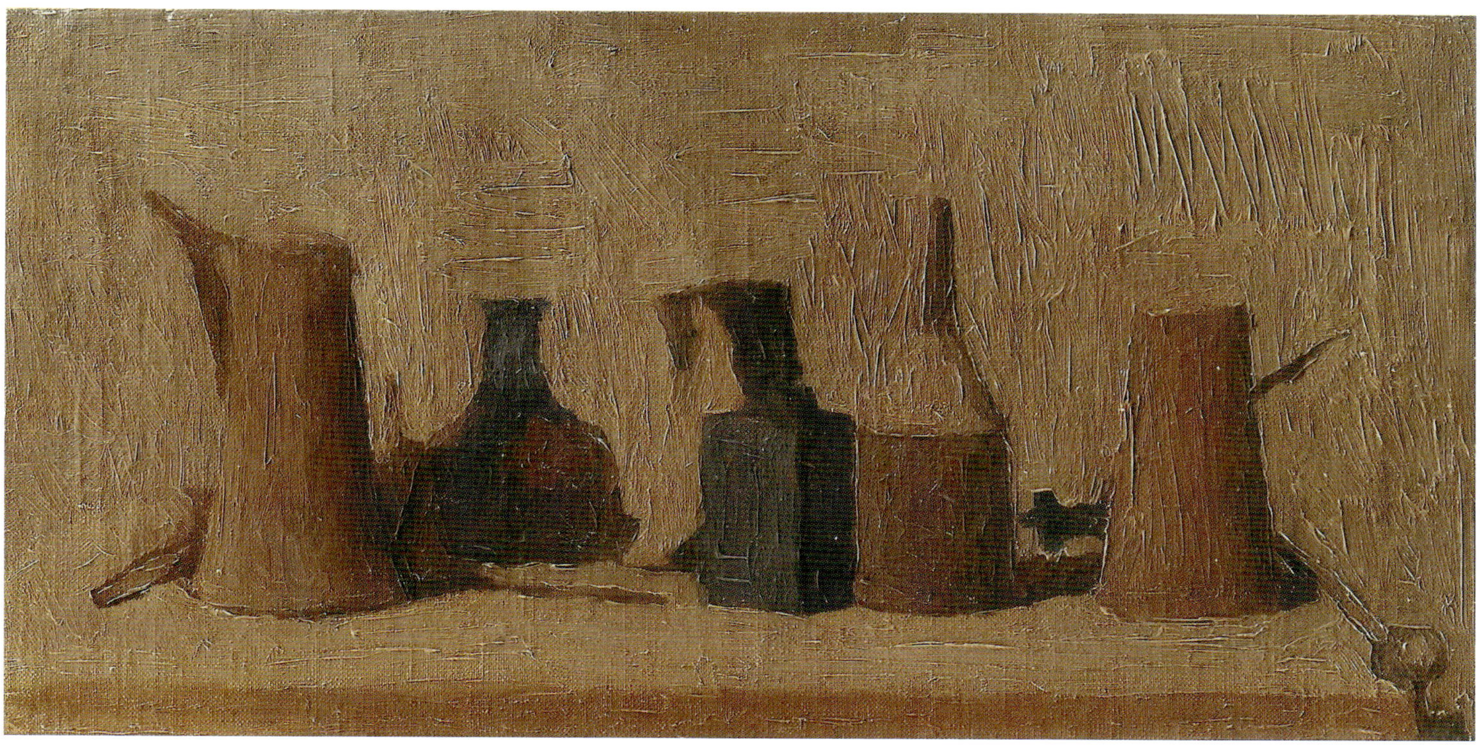

Paesaggio, 1932,
V. 174, oil on canvas, 50.5 × 60.5 cm
Courtesy Fondazione di Studi di Storia dell'Arte Roberto Longhi, Firenze

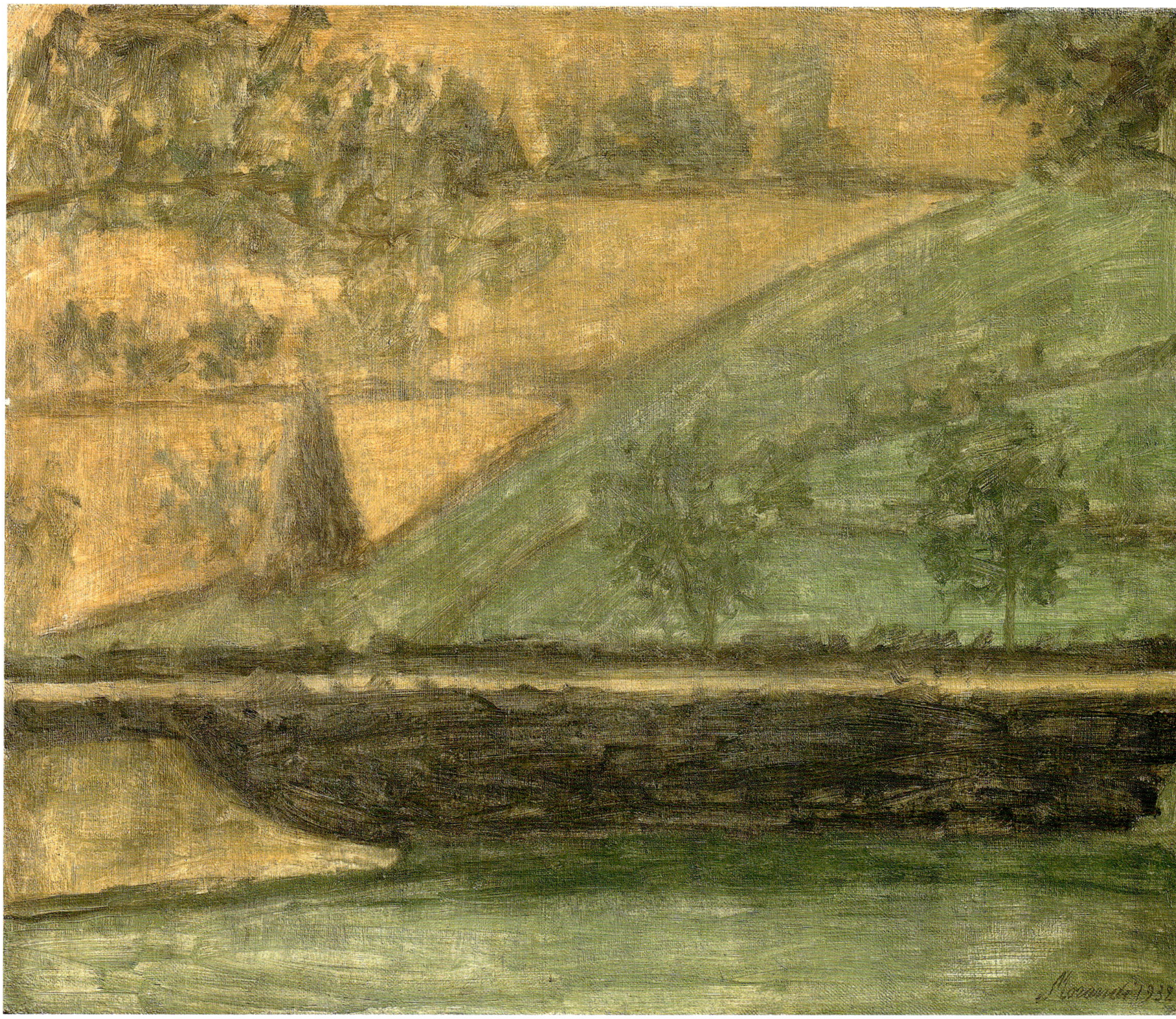

Paesaggio, 1934,
V. 181, oil on canvas, 63 × 76 cm
Courtesy Polo Museale della Toscana,
Collezione Cesare Brandi, Vignano

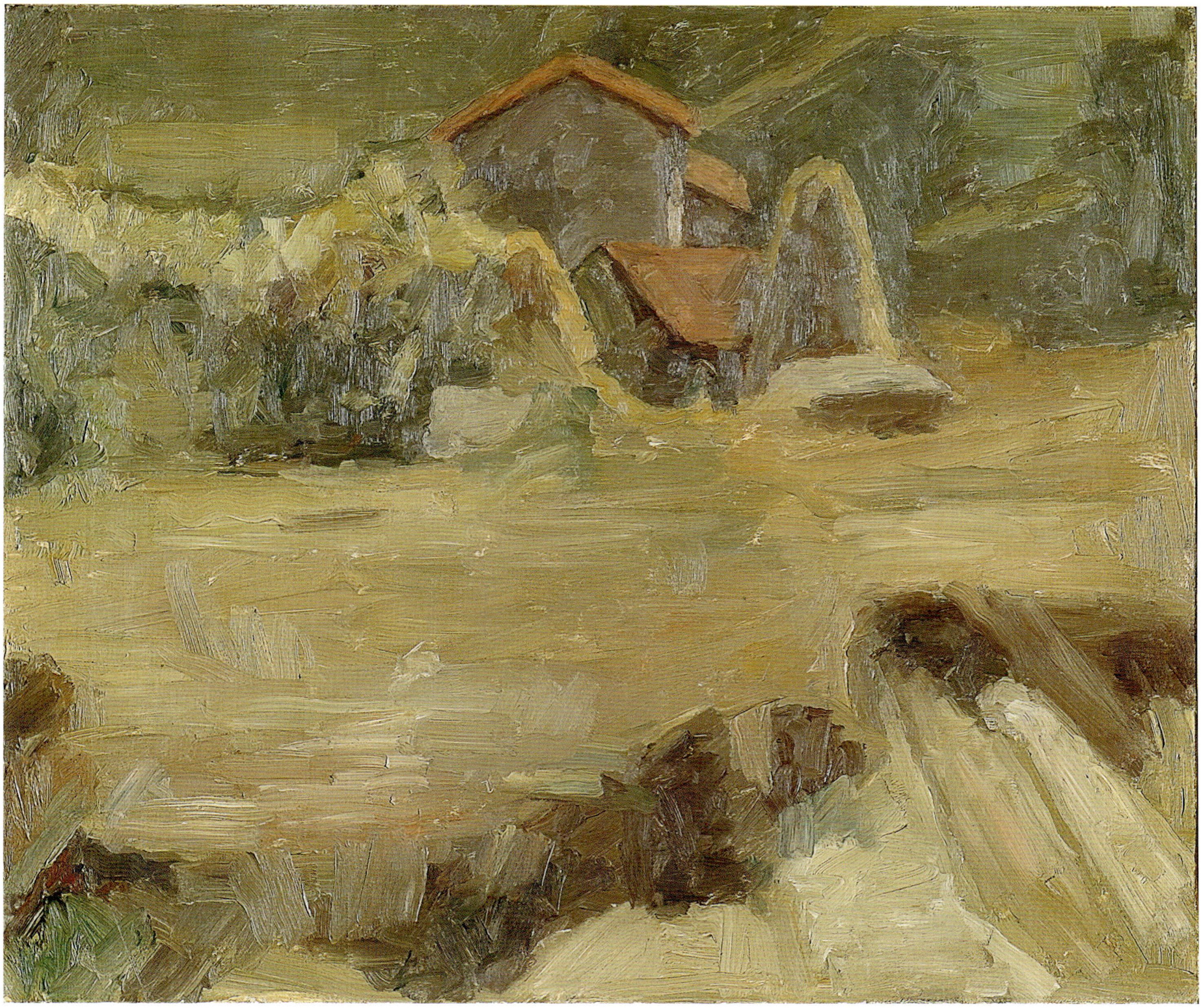

Paesaggio (cortile in via Fondazza), 1935,
V. 196, oil on canvas, 41 × 49 cm
Courtesy Collezione Giuseppe Merlini,
Busto Arsizio (VA)

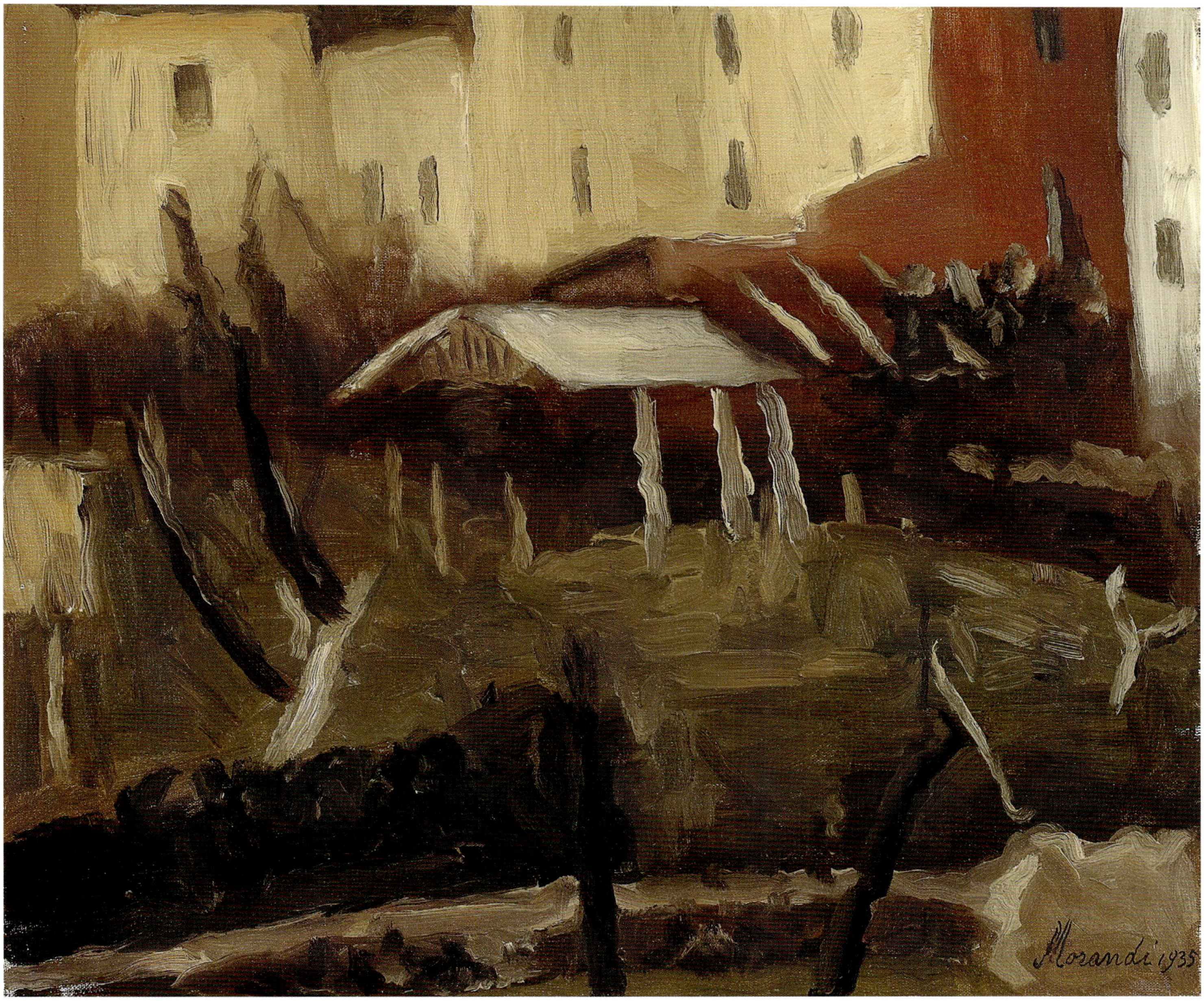
Morandi 1935

Paesaggio, 1936,
V. 213, oil on canvas, 60 × 60 cm
Courtesy Collezioni Civiche,
Raccolta Alberto Della Ragione, Firenze

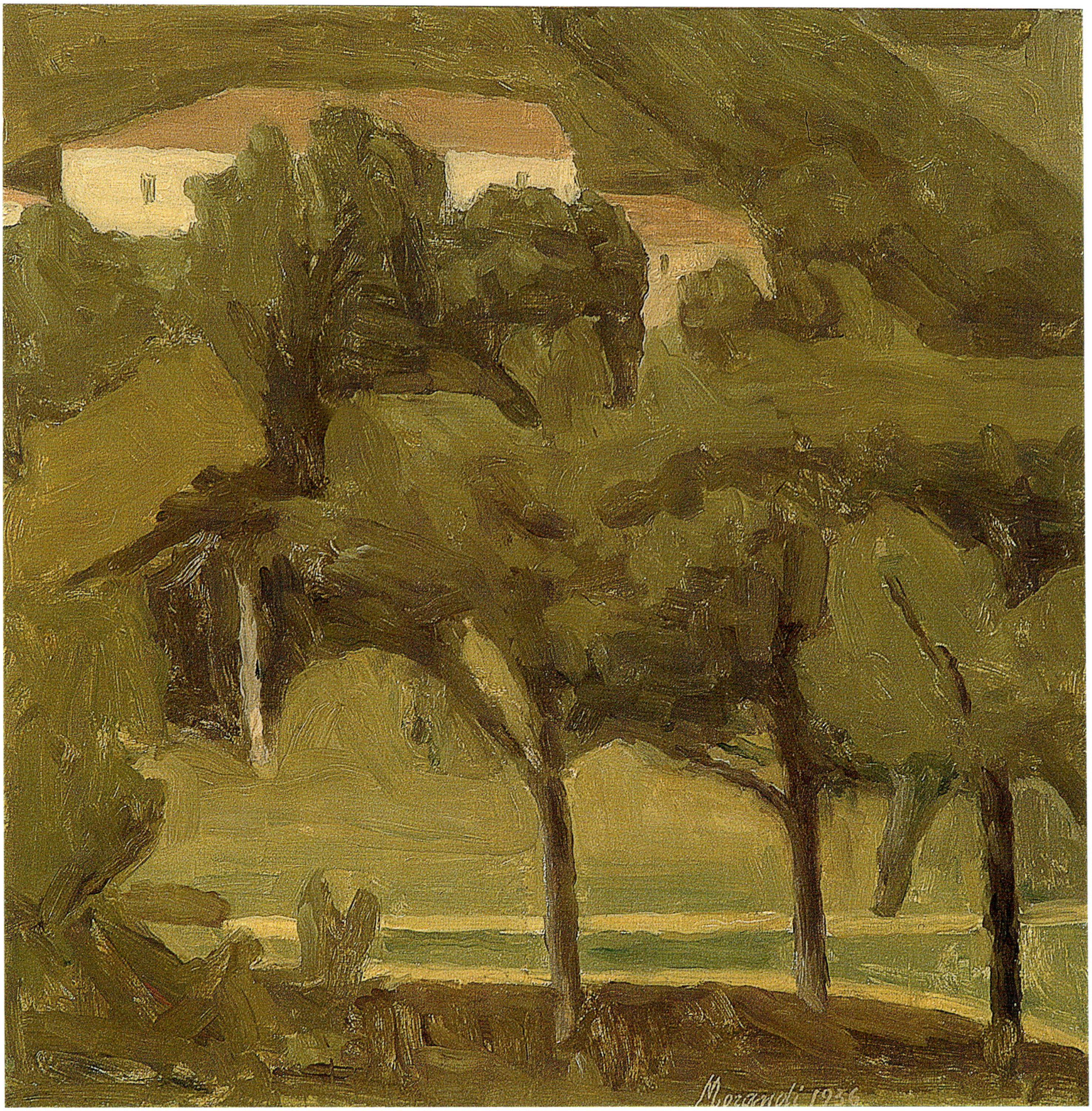

Natura morta (natura morta di oggetti in viola), 1937,
V. 222, oil on canvas, 61.8 × 76.3 cm
Courtesy Fondazione di Studi di Storia
dell'Arte Roberto Longhi, Firenze

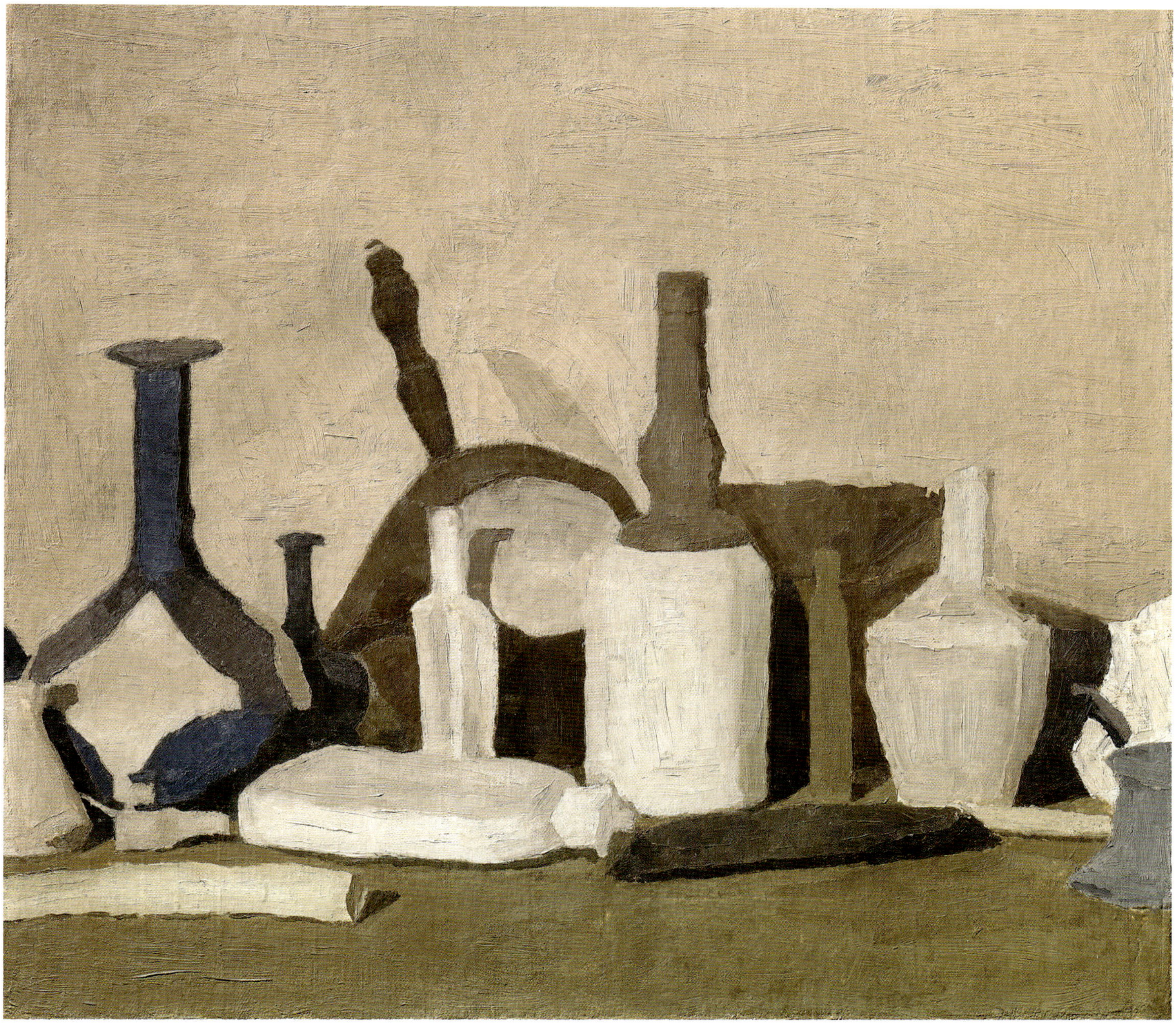

Natura morta, 1937 ca.-1938 ca.,
V. 232, oil on canvas, 42 × 63 cm
Courtesy Collezioni Civiche,
Raccolta Alberto Della Ragione, Firenze

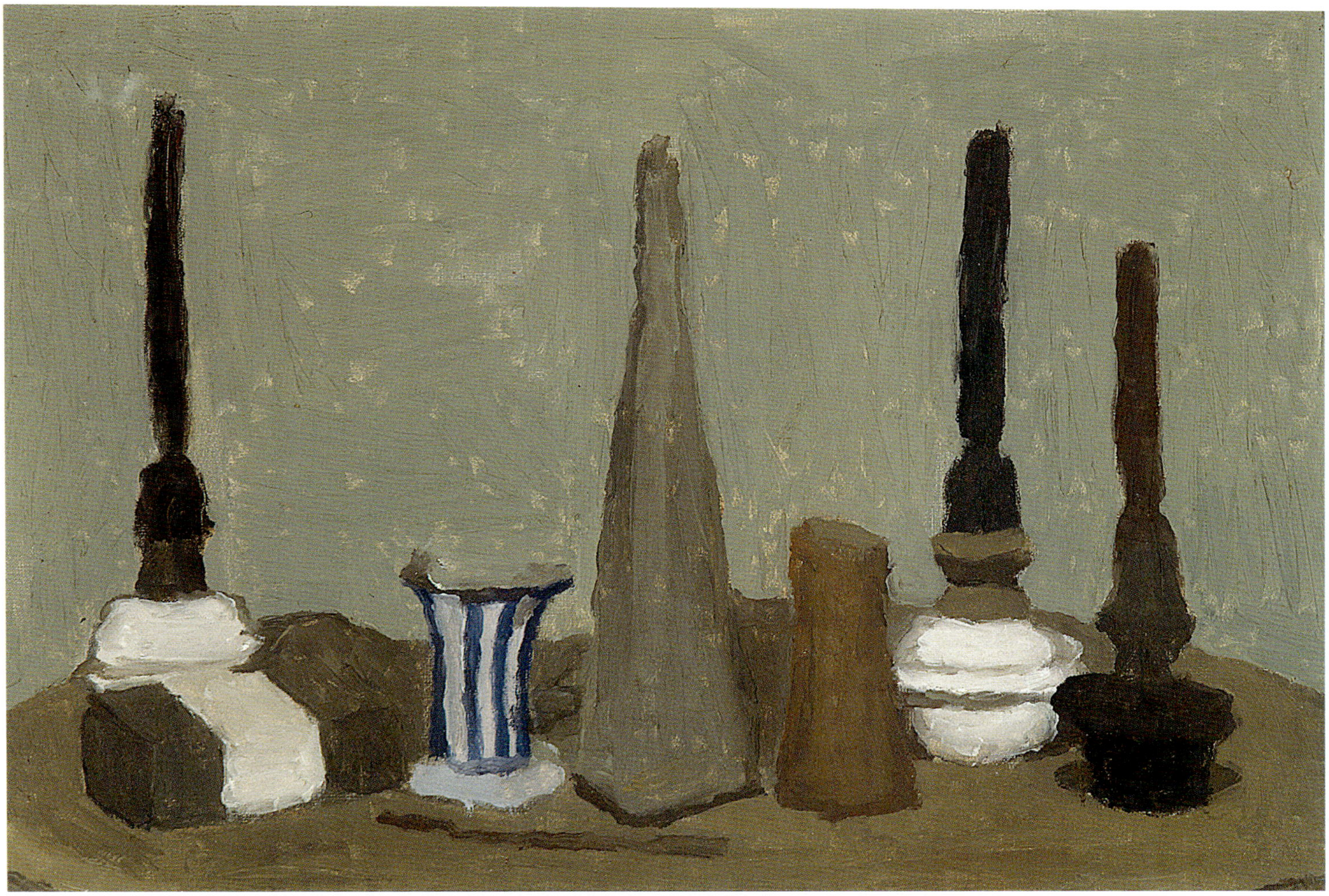

Paesaggio, 1940,
V. 277, oil on canvas, 34.5 × 31 cm
Courtesy Fondazione di Studi di Storia
dell'Arte Roberto Longhi, Firenze

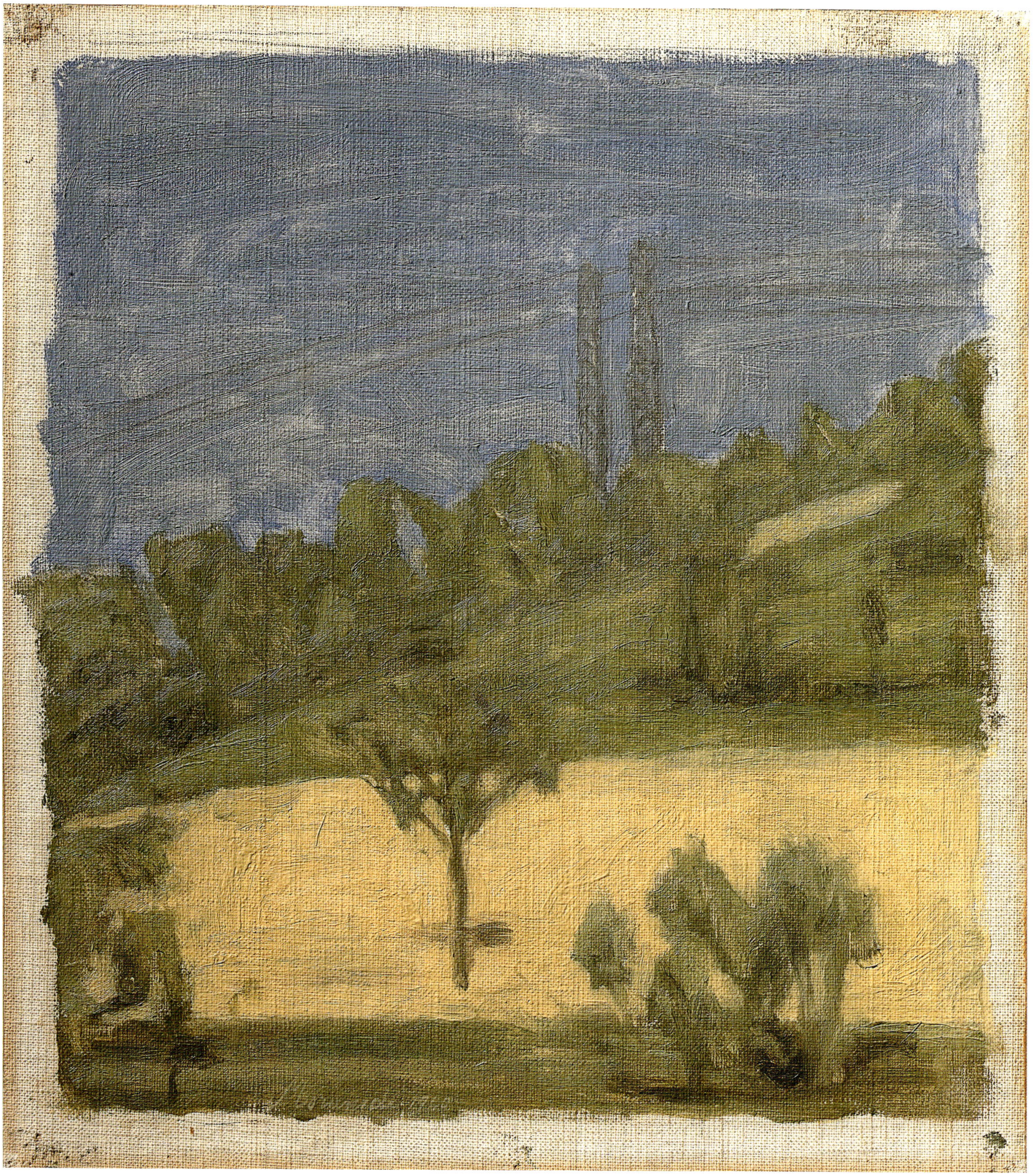

Paesaggio, 1941,
V. 389, oil on canvas, 49 × 49 cm
Courtesy Private Collection, Firenze

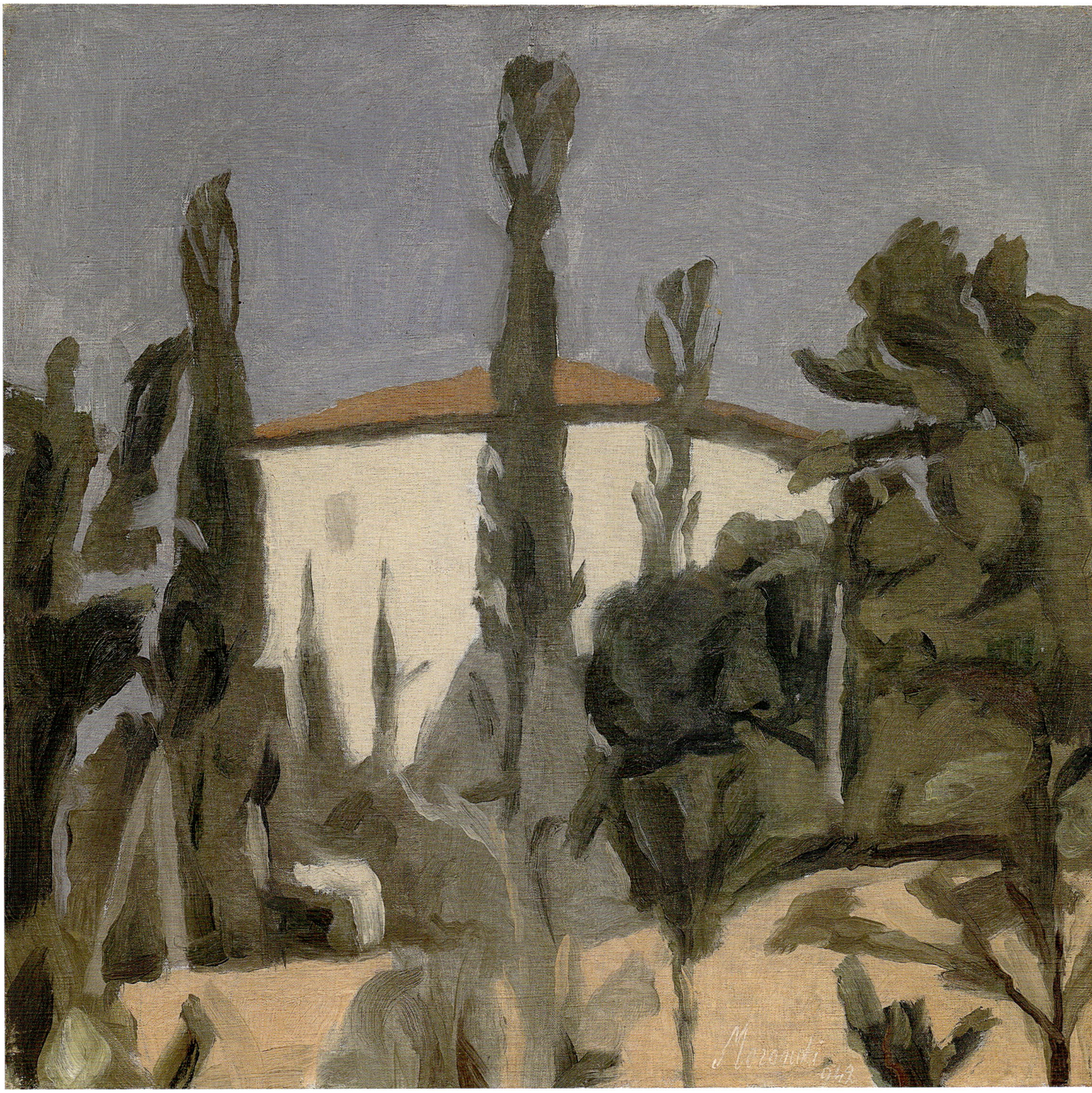

Paesaggio, 1941,
V. 342, oil on canvas, 41.5 × 52.7 cm
Courtesy Private Collection, Firenze

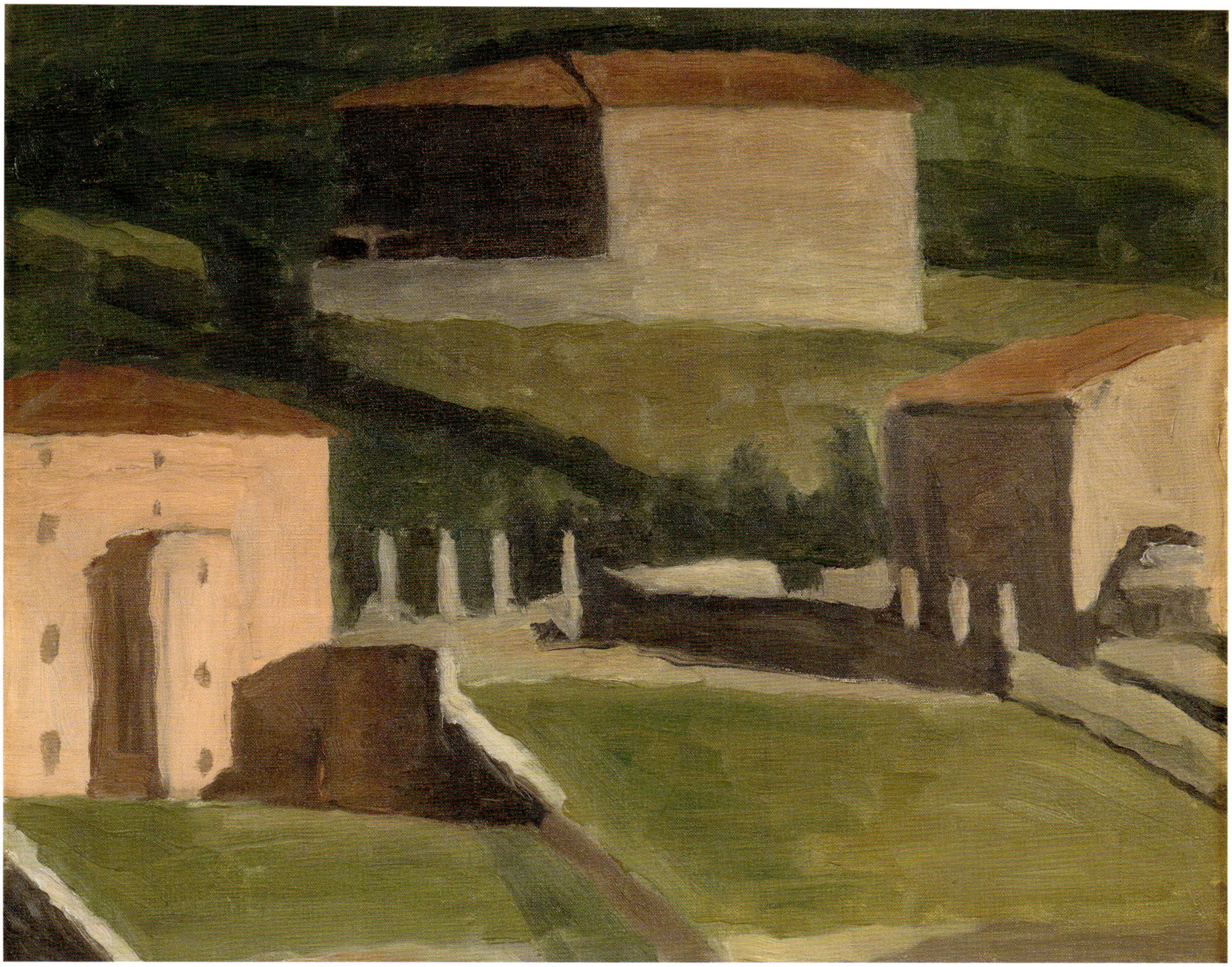

Natura morta, 1941,
V. 314, oil on canvas, 31 × 46 cm
Courtesy Private Collection, Firenze

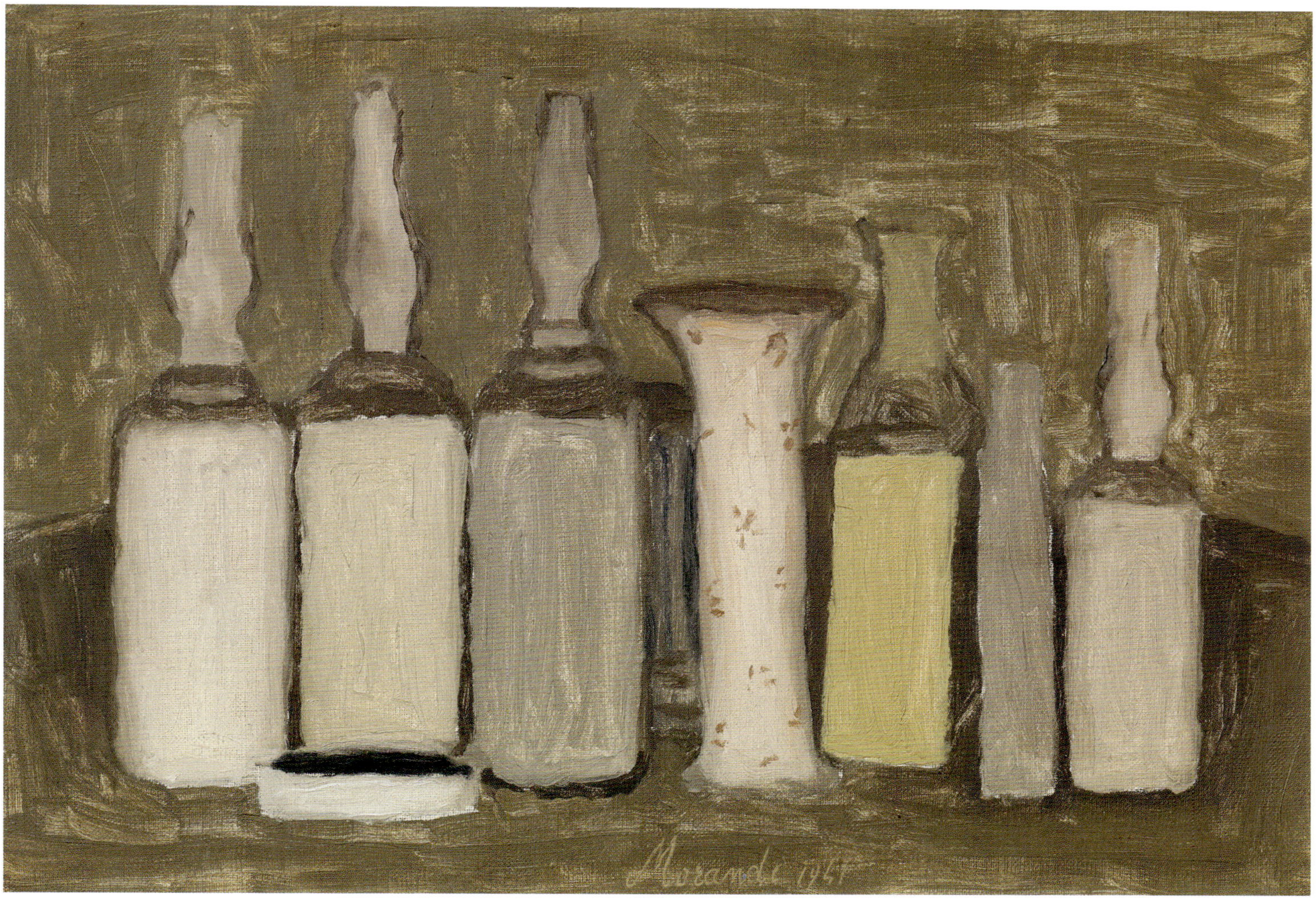

Natura morta, 1942,
P. 2000, p. 187, oil on canvas, 35 × 50 cm
Courtesy Elisabetta Fabbri e Franco Faldi

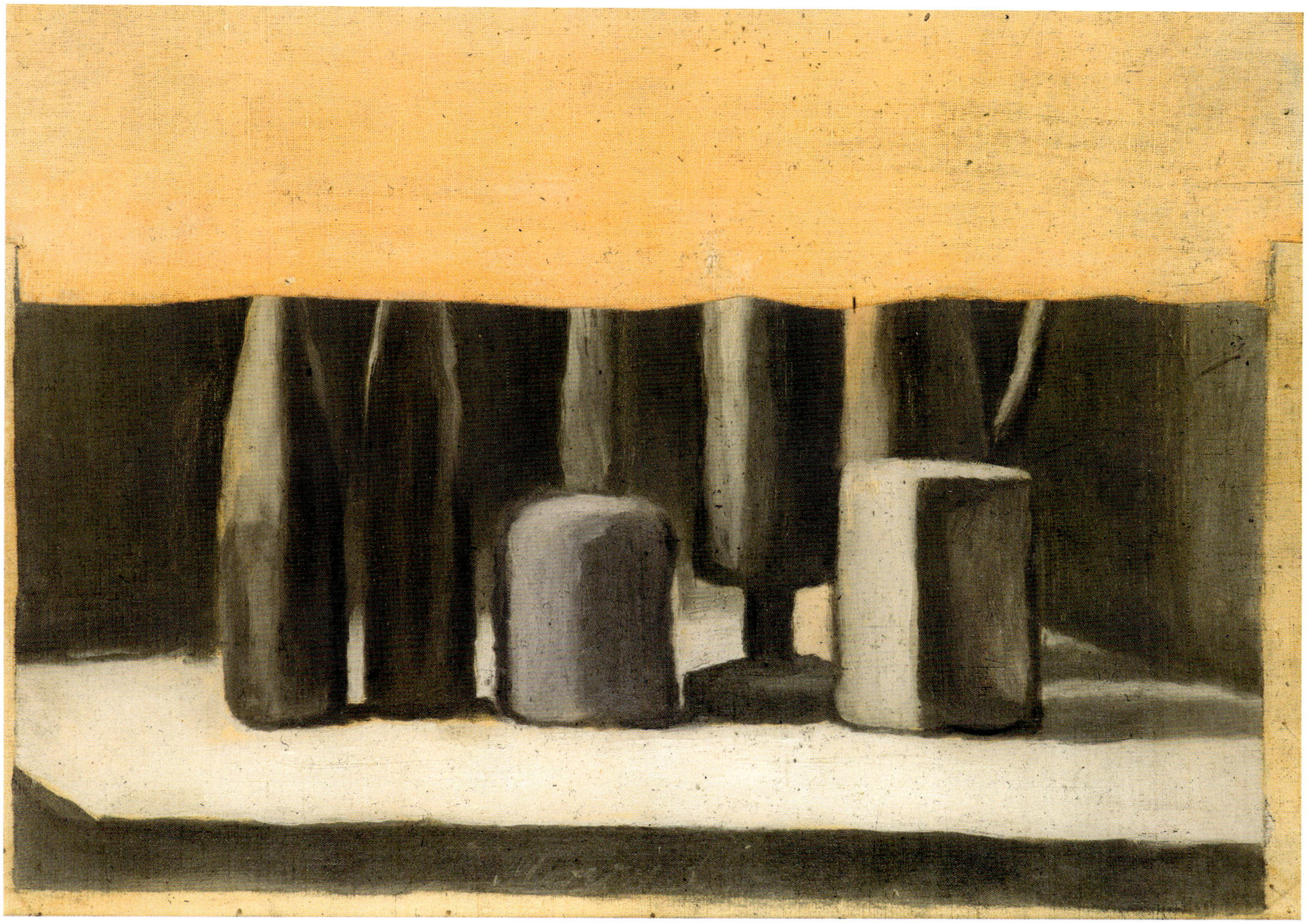

Fiori, 1943,
V. 408, oil on canvas, 20.7 × 25.3 cm
Courtesy Fondazione di Studi di Storia
dell'Arte Roberto Longhi, Firenze

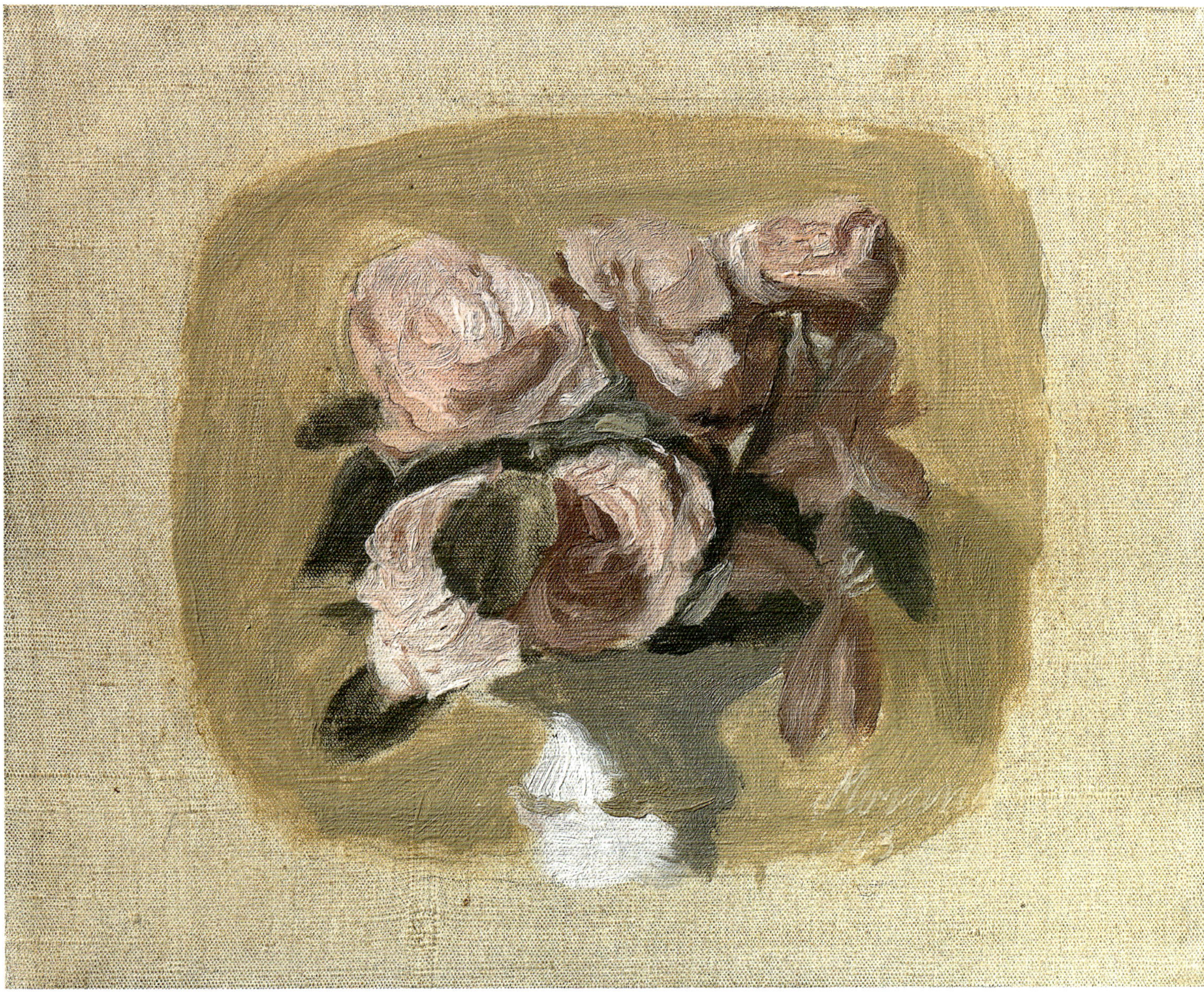

Paesaggio, 1943,
V. 454, oil on canvas, 41.5 × 53 cm
Courtesy Collezione Banca Monte
dei Paschi di Siena

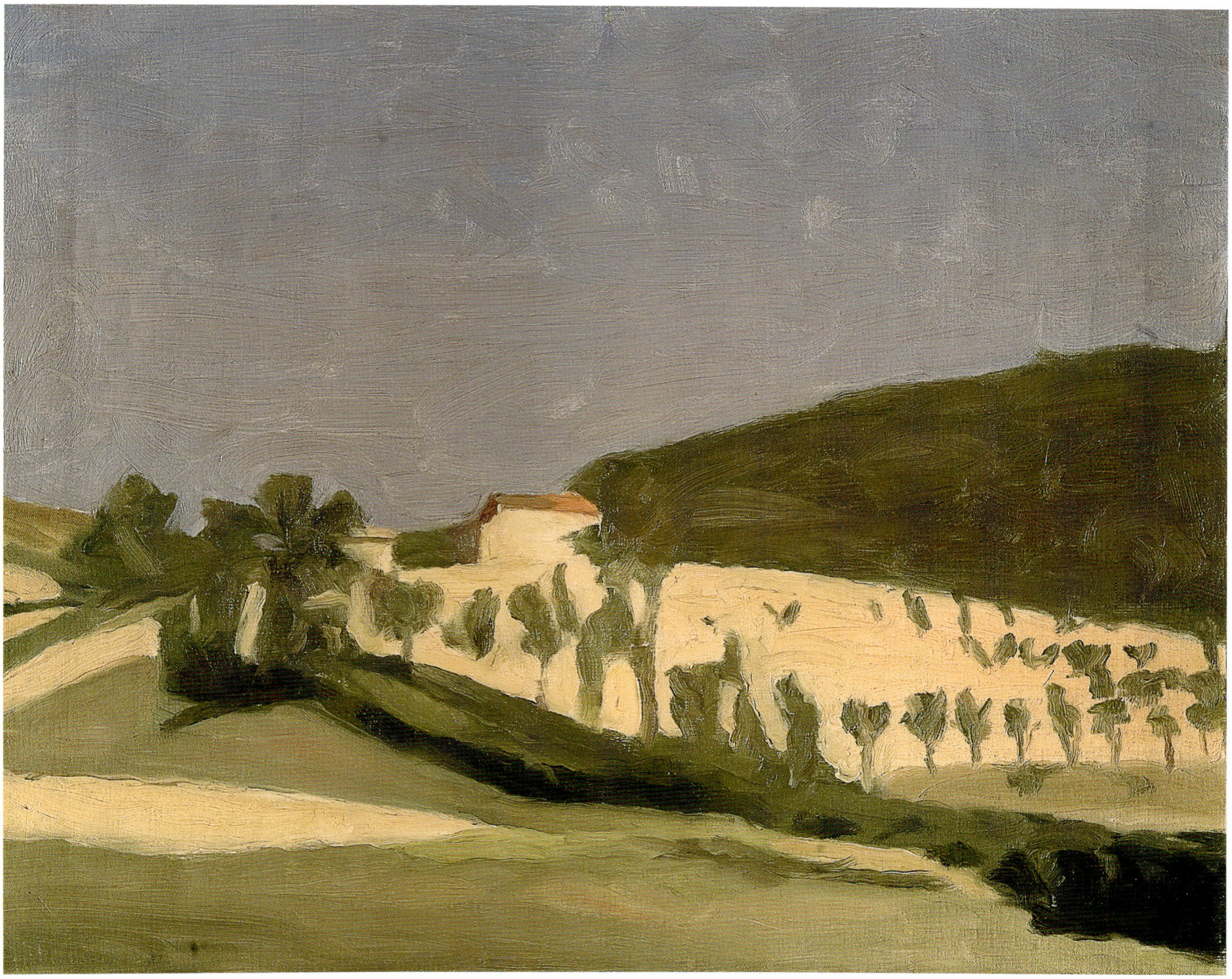

Natura morta, 1948,
V. 612, oil on canvas, 26 × 36.3 cm
Courtesy Collezione Gori, Pistoia

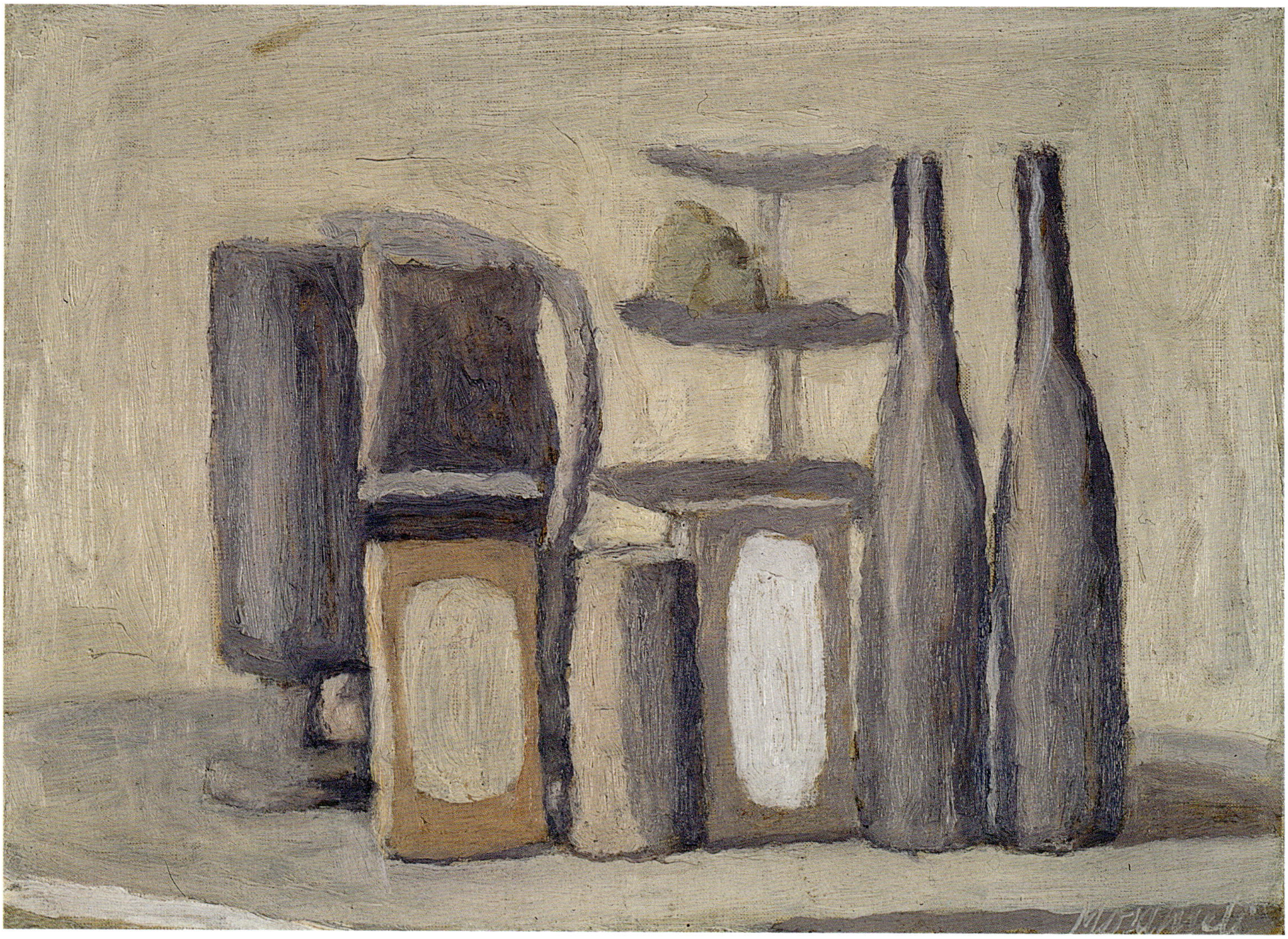

Natura morta, 1954,
V. 906, oil on canvas, 31.2 × 36.3 cm
Courtesy Fondazione di Studi di Storia dell'Arte Roberto Longhi, Firenze

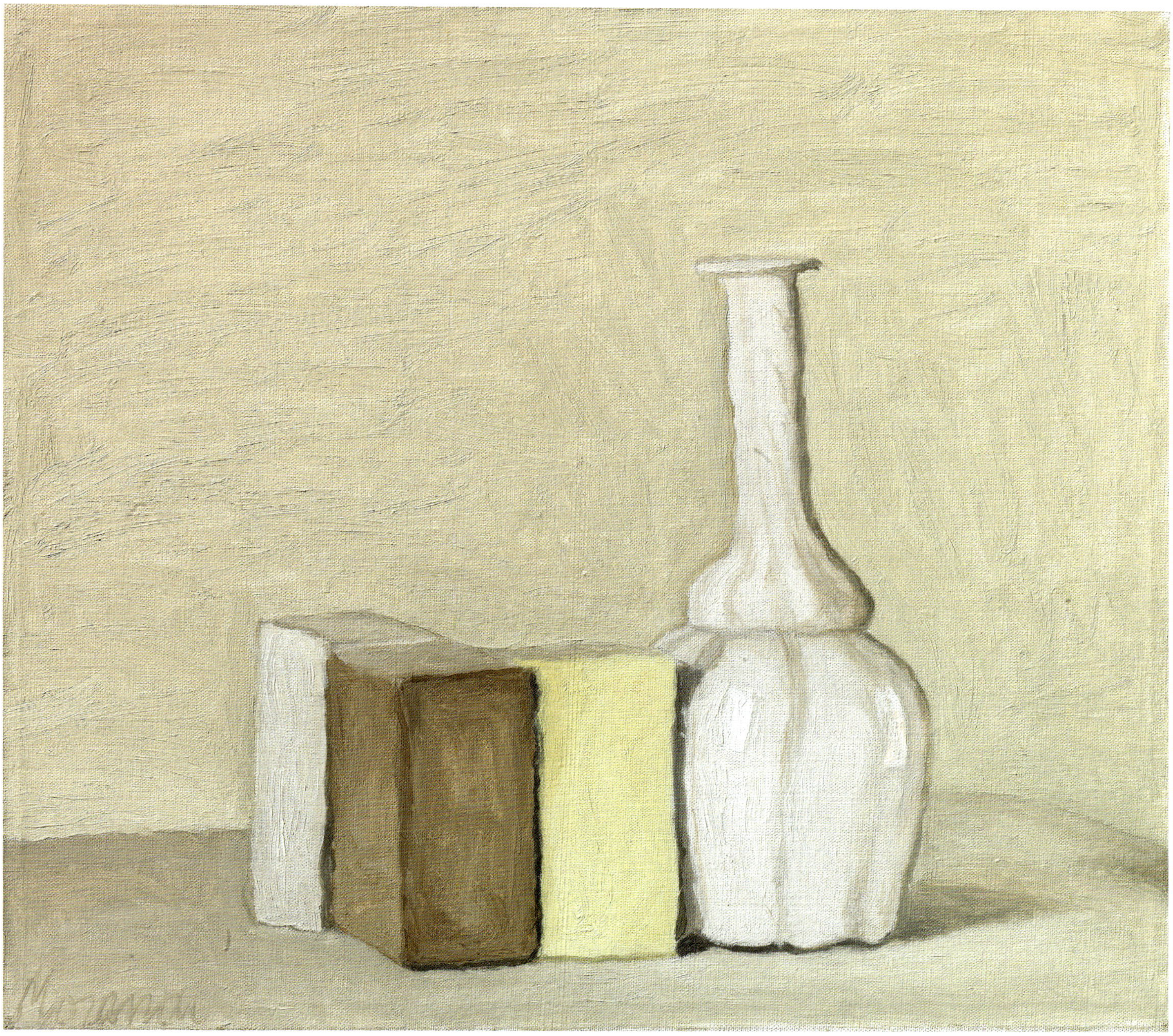

Natura morta, 1956,
V. 1005, oil on canvas, 4.5 × 4.5 cm
Courtesy Collezione Banca
Monte dei Paschi di Siena

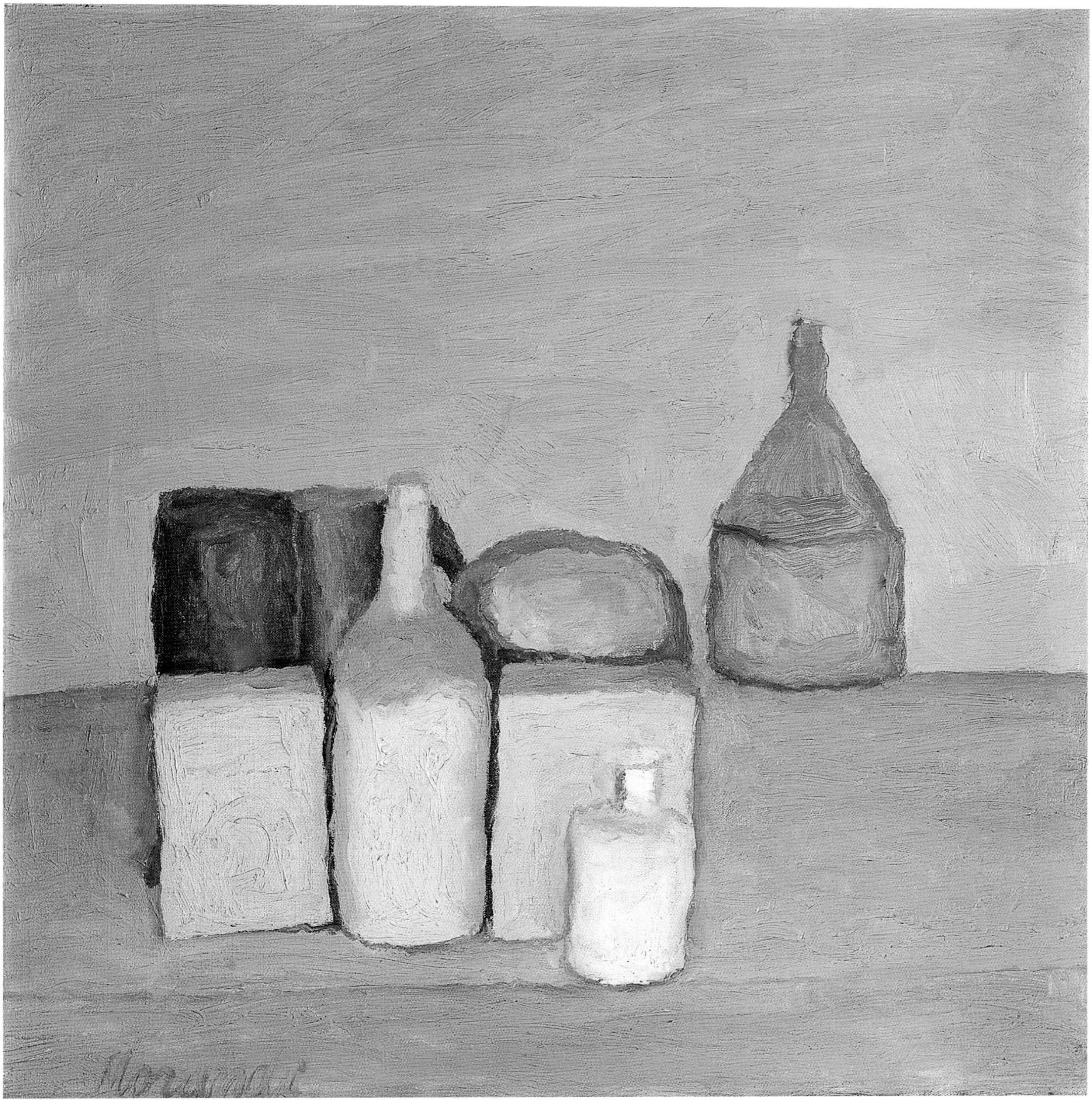

Natura morta, 1957 ca.,
V. 1057, oil on canvas, 36.5 × 46.5 cm
Courtesy Polo Museale della Toscana,
Collezione Cesare Brandi, Vignano

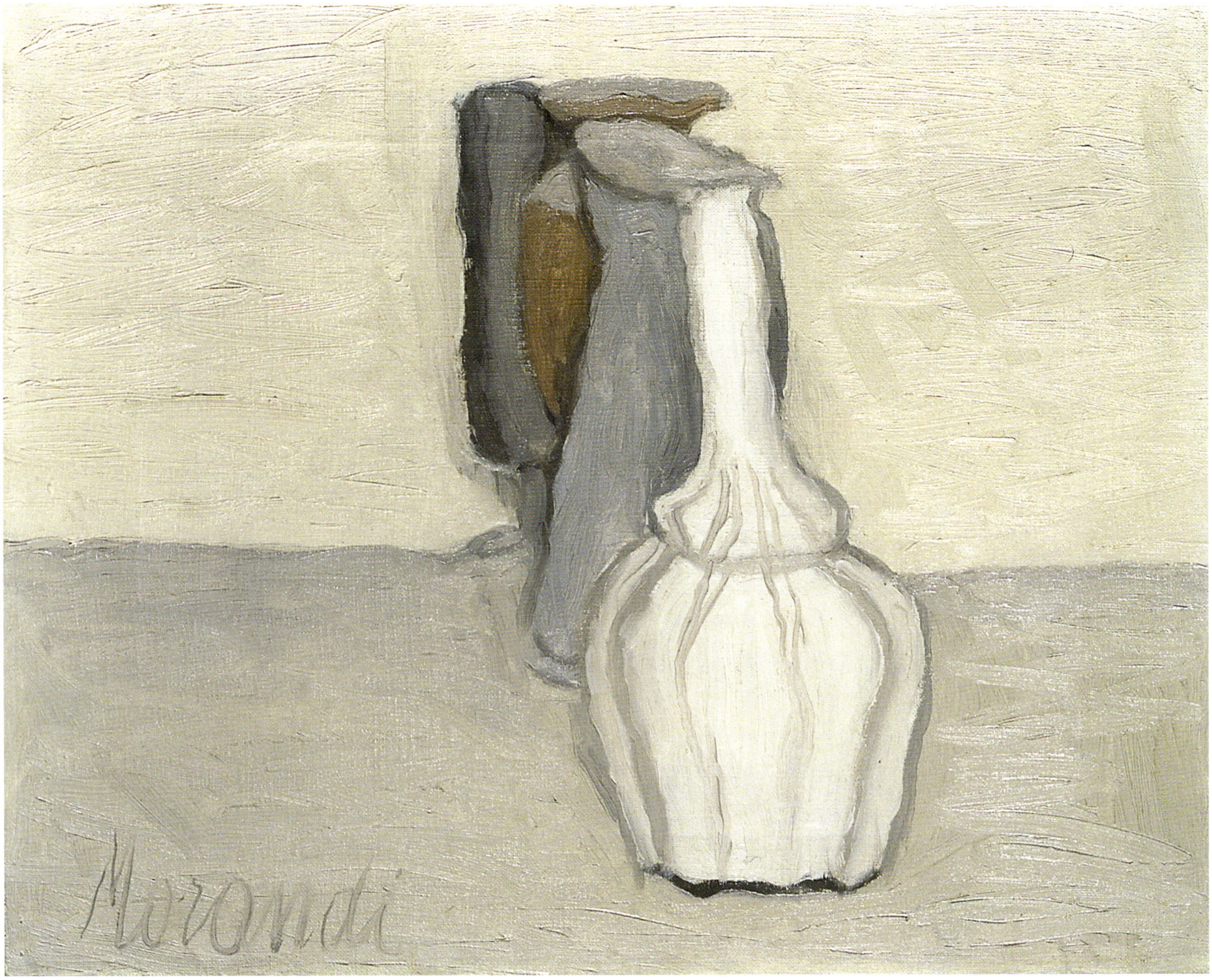
Morandi

Natura morta, T.P. 1932/7,
silverpoint on paper, 163 × 233 mm
Courtesy Galleria Nazionale d'Arte
Moderna e Contemporanea, Roma

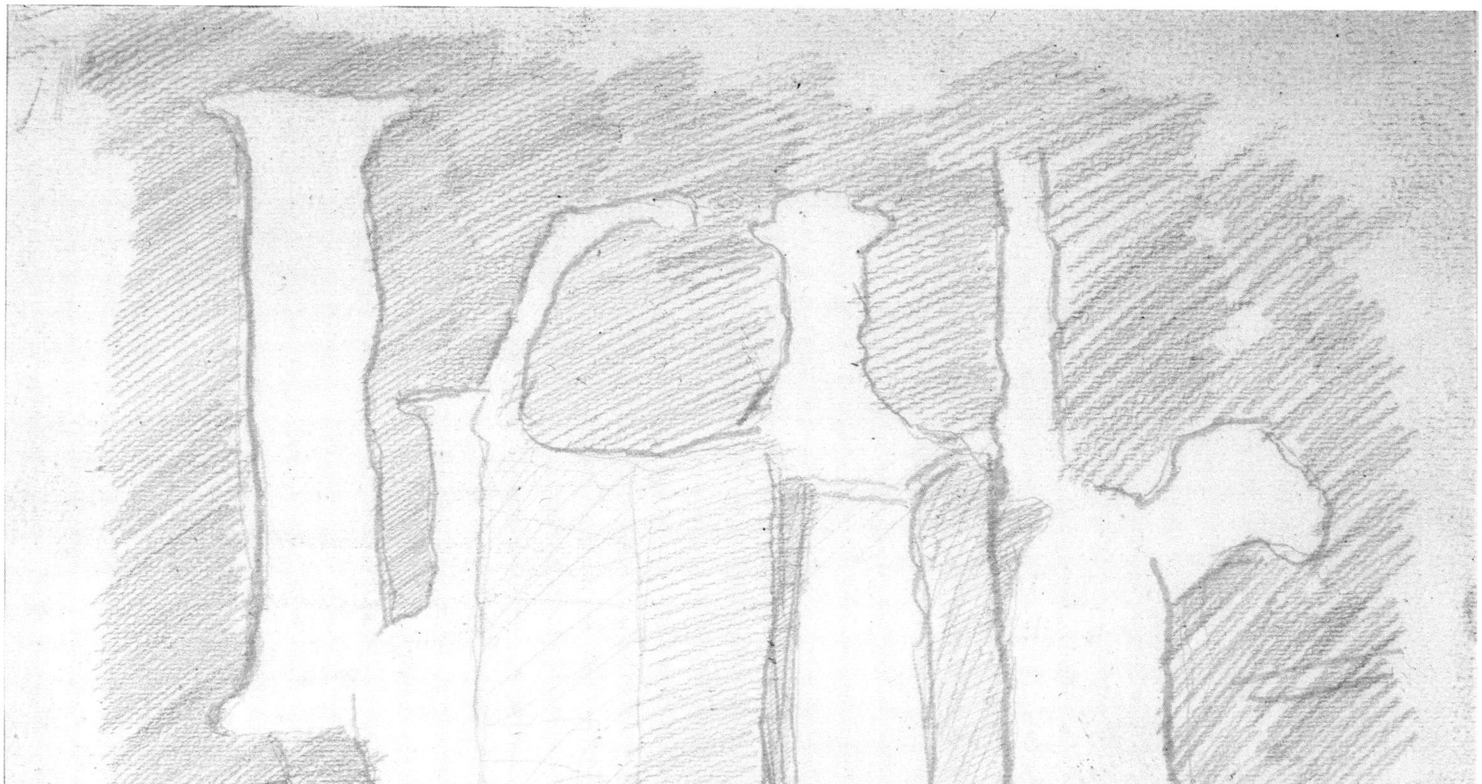
Morandi 1932

Fiori, T.P. 1939/1,
pencil on paper, 270 × 190 mm
Courtesy Galleria Nazionale d'Arte
Moderna e Contemporanea, Roma

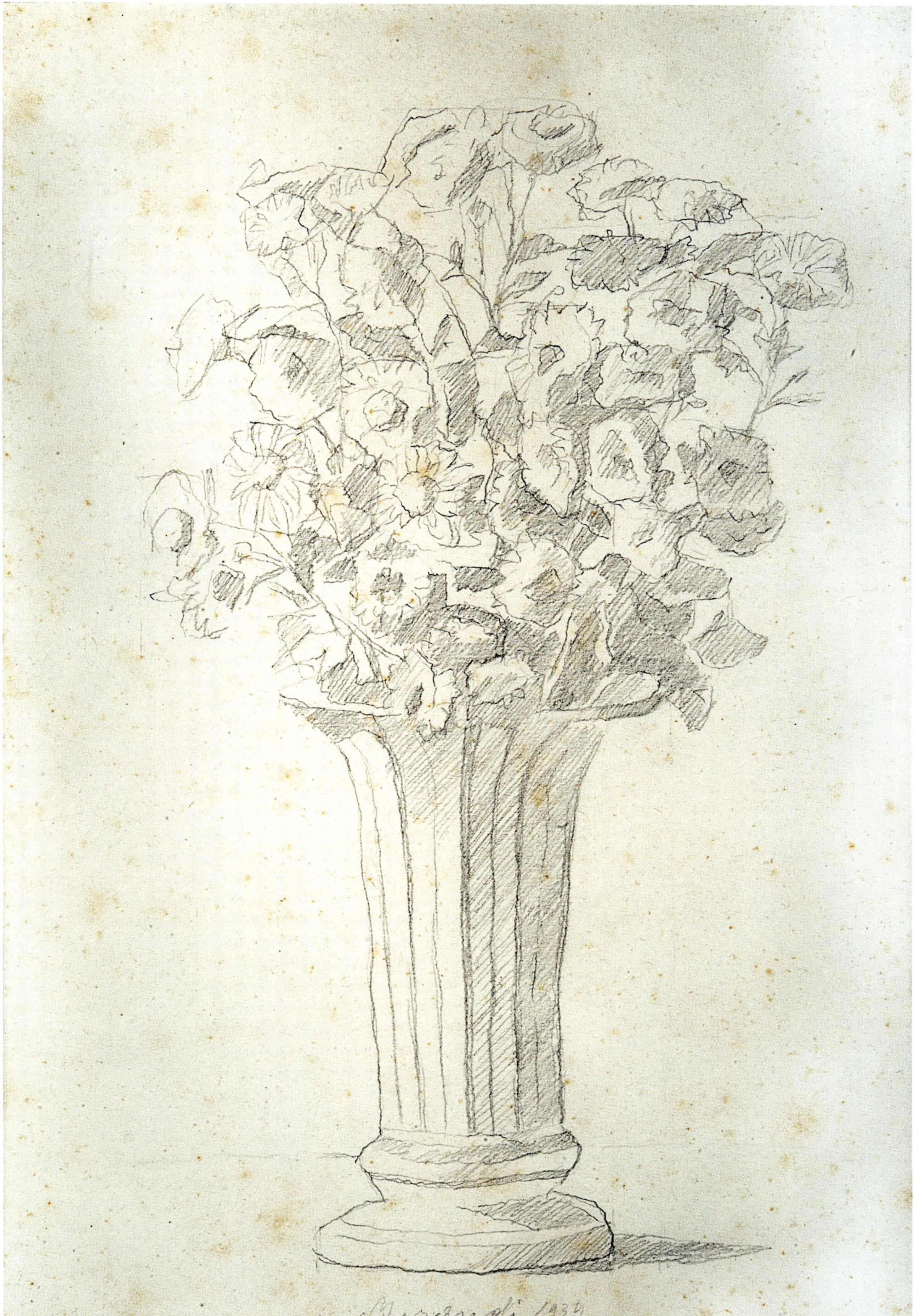
Morandi 1939

Paesaggio (veduta dell'Osservanza a Bologna), 1921, V. inc. 16, etching on ivory paper, 184 × 248 mm (paper), 72 × 123 mm (engraved part).
Courtesy Fondazione di Studi di Storia dell'Arte Roberto Longhi, Firenze

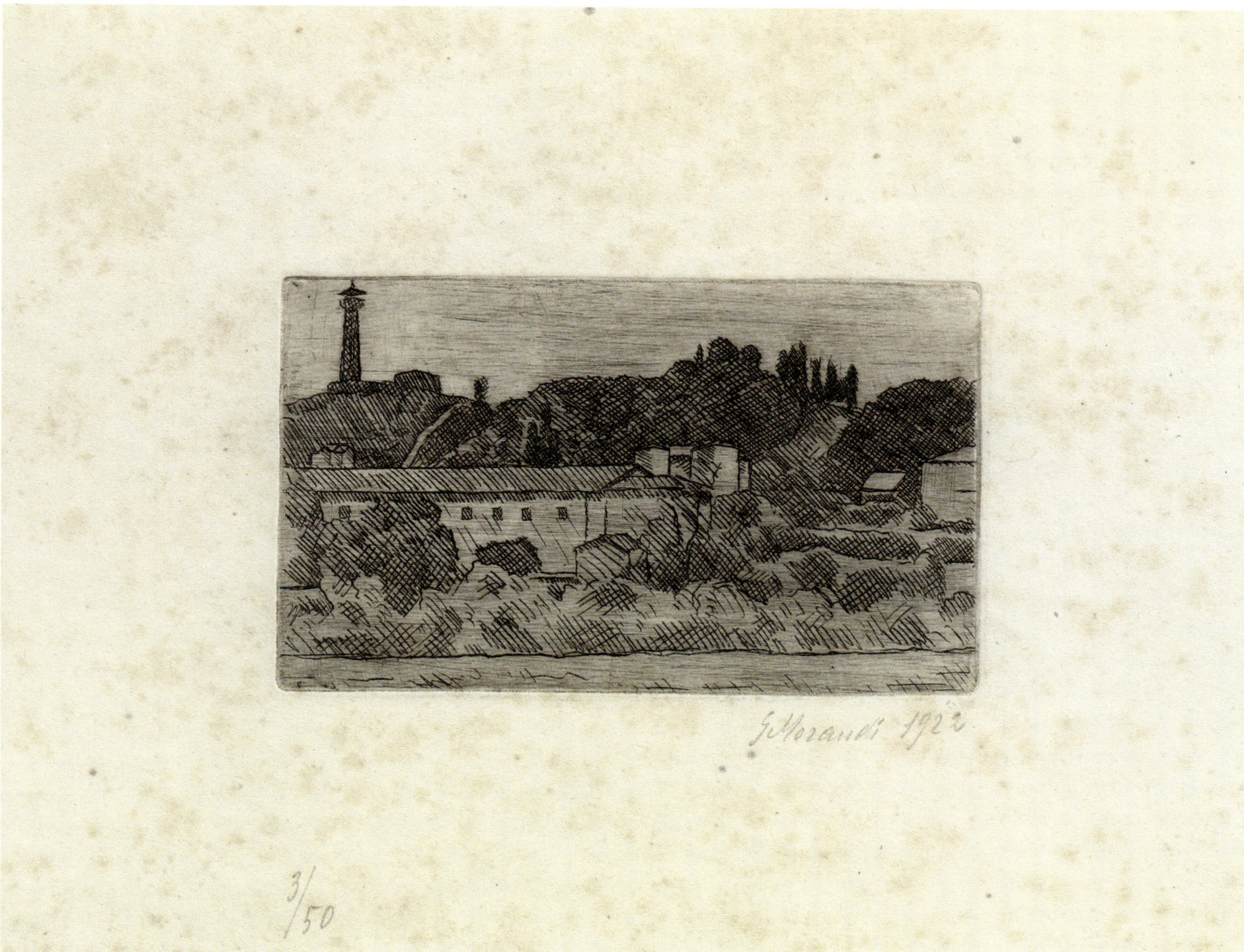
G. Morandi 1922
3/50

Natura morta con la statuina, 1922,
V. inc. 17, etching on ivory paper,
125 × 132 mm (paper), 60 × 70 mm (engraved part).
Courtesy Fondazione di Studi di Storia
dell'Arte Roberto Longhi, Firenze

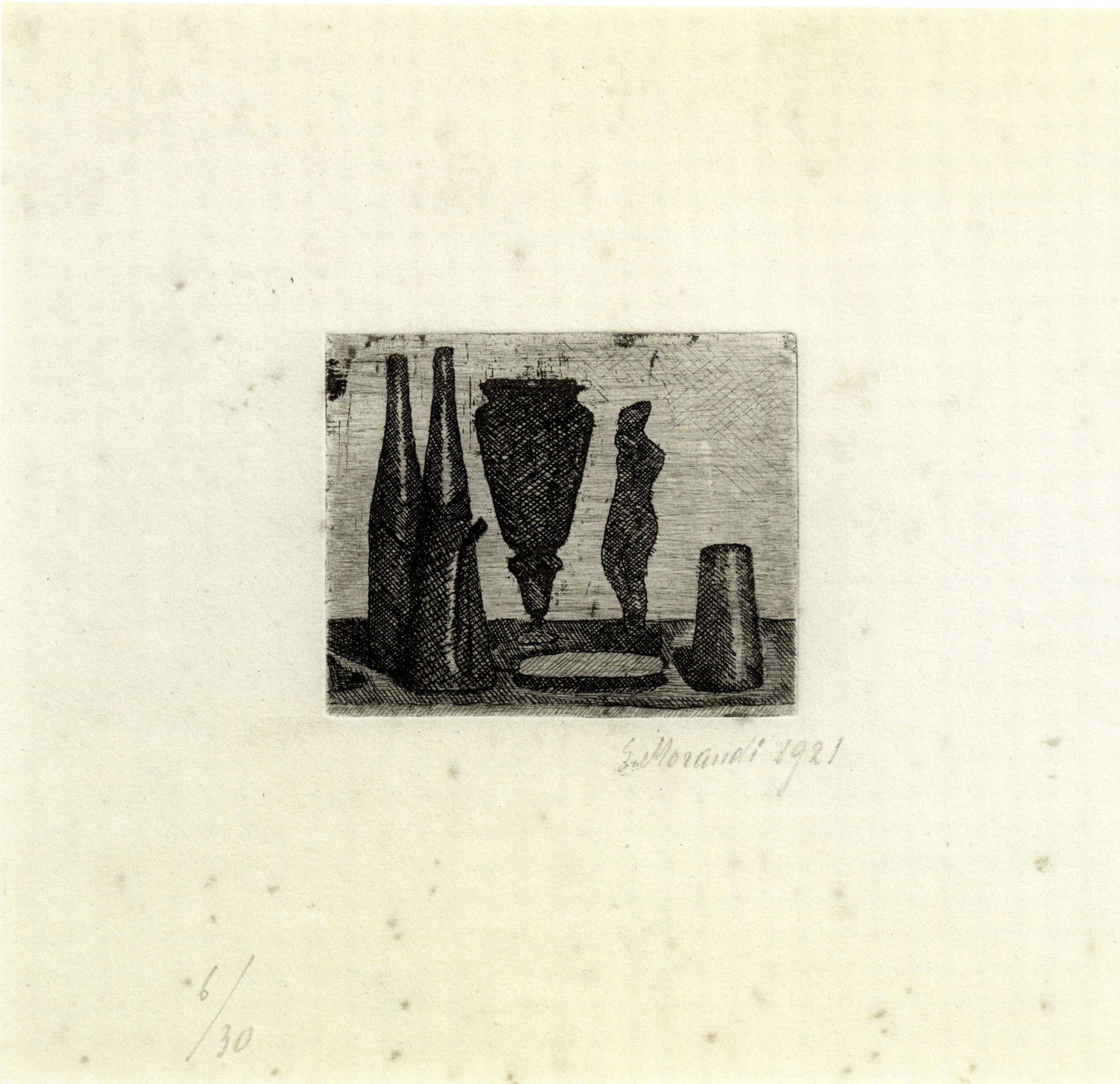
G. Morandi 1921
6/30

Paesaggio con la ciminiera (sobborghi di Bologna), 1926, V. inc. 27, etching on ivory paper, 381 × 510 mm (paper), 227 × 241 mm (engraved part).
Courtesy Fondazione di Studi di Storia dell'Arte Roberto Longhi, Firenze

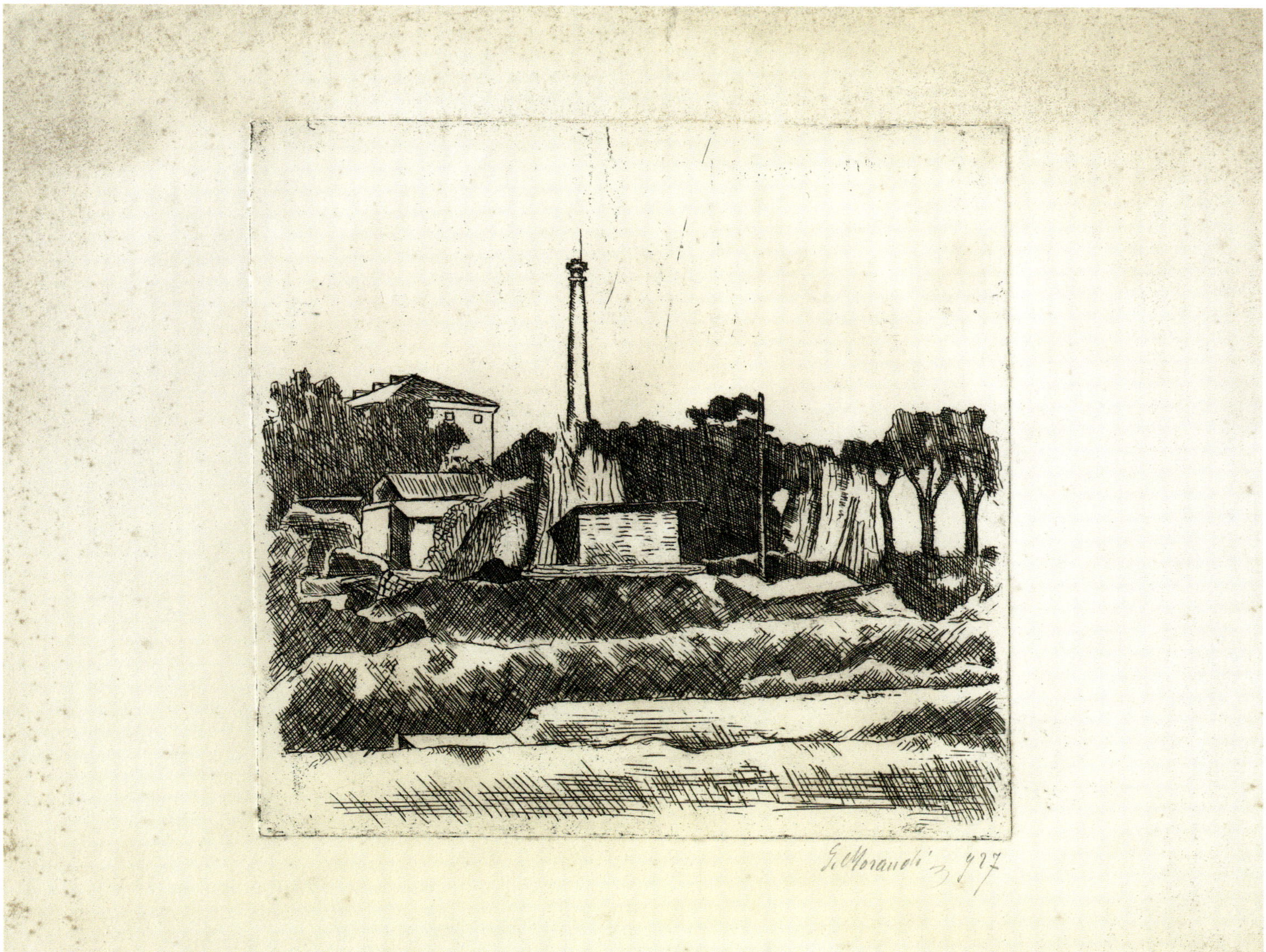

Natura morta con compostiera e lume a petrolio, 1930 ca.,
V. inc. 137, etching on zinc, 310 × 410 mm
Courtesy Collezione Banca Monte dei Paschi di Siena

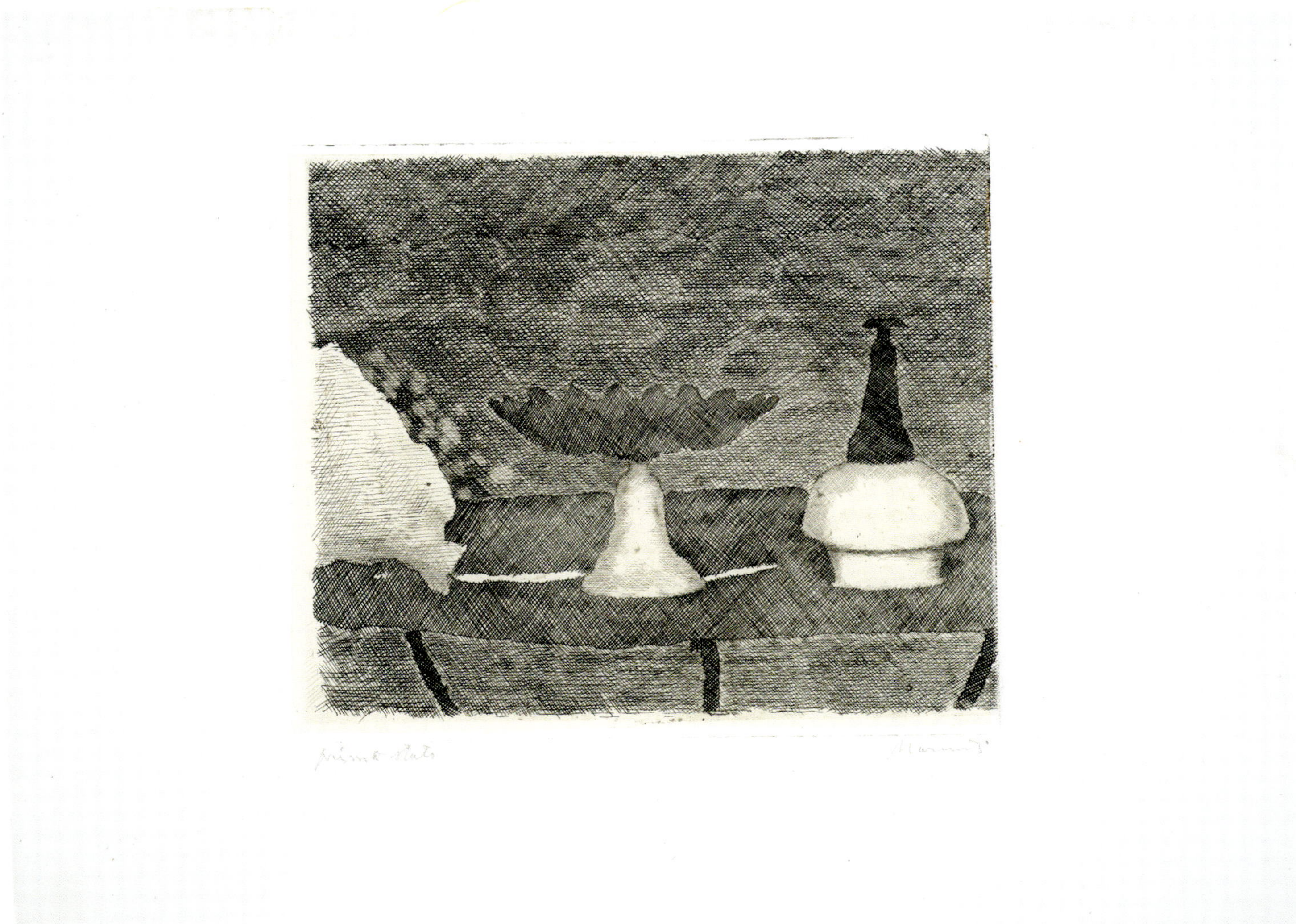
primo stato
Morandi

Natura morta in un tondo, 1942,
V. inc. 109, etching on paper, 377 × 45 mm
Courtesy Collezione Banca Monte dei Paschi di Siena

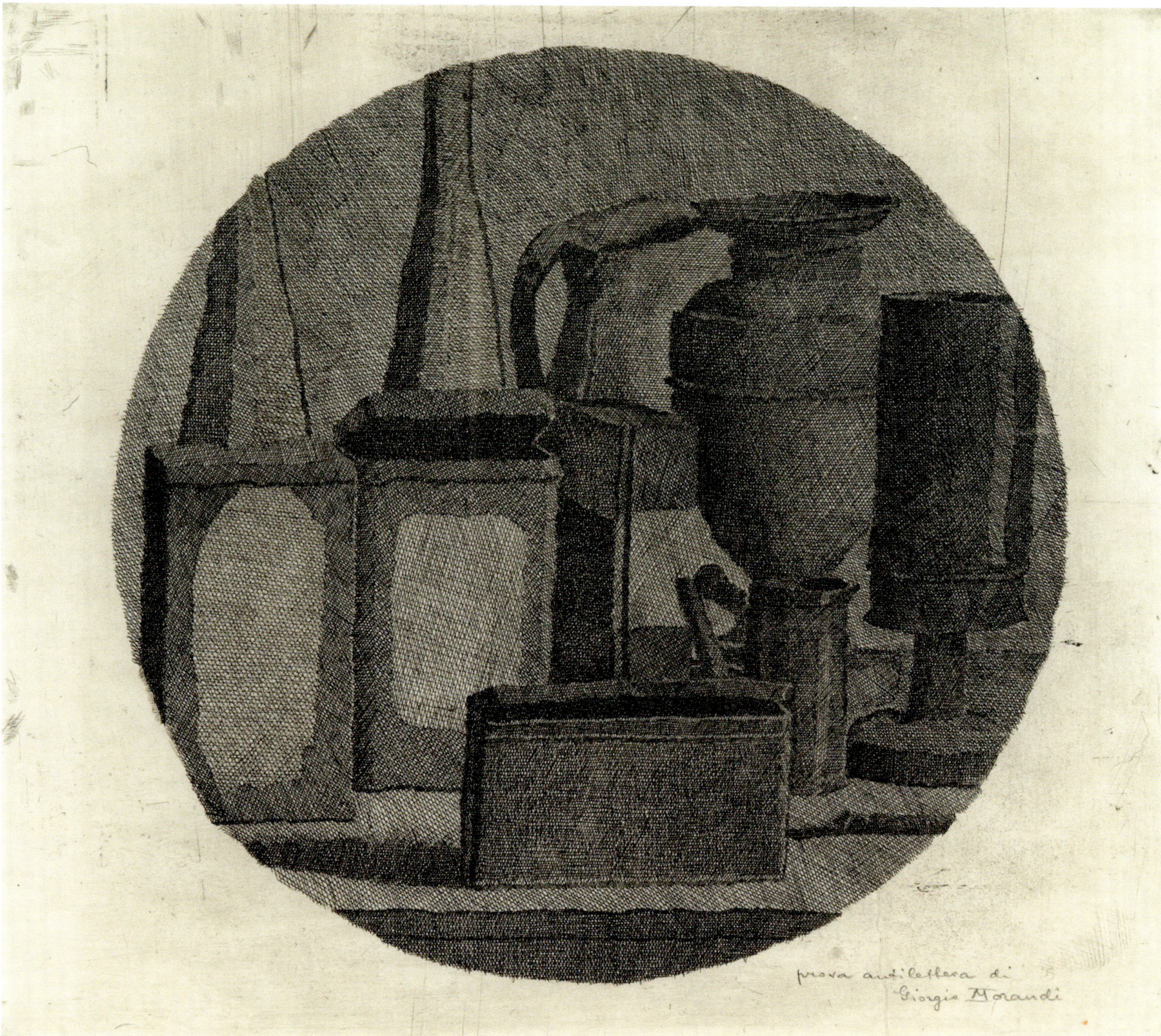
prova antilettera di
Giorgio Morandi

Biographical Outline

Maria Cristina Bandera

1890
Birth of Giorgio Morandi, the first of five sons, in Bologna on July 20.

1907
Enrollment at the Bologna Accademia di Belle Arti and attendance until 1913.

1909
Meeting with Osvaldo Licini, a fellow student at the academy. Visit to the VIII Venice Biennale. Studies paintings by Cézanne for the first time in reproductions in Vittorio Pica's *Gl'Impressionisti francesi* (1908). Reads Ardengo Soffici's articles in the magazine *La Voce*.

1910
Visit to the IX Venice Biennale. The works seen include the whole room of paintings by Renoir. A trip to Florence provides an opportunity to study Giotto, Masaccio, and Paolo Uccello.

1911
Sees original works by Monet for the first time at the World's Fair in Rome. Date of the earliest surviving painting (*Paesaggio* V. 2).

1912
First known etching (*Il ponte sul Savena a Bologna*, V.inc.1).

1913
Graduates at the academy and paints the first landscapes at Grizzana. Meets the writer Riccardo Bacchelli and his brother Mario, the painter. Present at the Serata Futurista [Futurist soirée] in Modena in the spring.

1914
Visits the exhibition of futurist painting organized in Florence by the magazine *Lacerba* in January. Attends the futurist soirée at the Teatro del Corso in Bologna, where he meets Umberto Boccioni and Carlo Carrà. Takes part in a one-day show at the Baglioni Hotel in Bologna on March 20 together with Mario Bacchelli, Osvaldo Licini, Severo Pozzati, and Giacomo Vespignani.
Takes part in the *Prima Esposizione Libera Futurista* at the Galleria Sprovieri, Rome, and then in the *Seconda Esposizione della Secessione*, where he has the opportunity to see a selection of watercolors by Cézanne and some paintings by Matisse.
Studies Giotto in Assisi and then in Padua.
Begins to teach drawing in elementary schools, a job continued until 1930.

1915
Called up for service (because of his height) in the Second Regiment of Grenadiers, but falls seriously ill and is declared definitively unfit.

1916
Spends the summer at Tolè di Vergato in the Emilian Apennines and devotes himself to painting.

1917
Paints fewer works due to serious illness.

1918
Reproduction of the etching *Natura morta con bottiglia e brocca* (1915, V.inc.3) published in Giuseppe Raimondi's magazine *La Raccolta* (Bologna).
Introduced to the metaphysical works of Giorgio de Chirico and Carlo Carrà in reproductions by his friend Raimondi. Paints his first 'metaphysical' works.
Meeting with Mario Broglio, who founds the magazine *Valori Plastici* in the same year. Riccardo Bacchelli publishes the first critique of his work in the daily paper *Il Tempo*.

1919
First paintings published in *La Raccolta* and *Valori Plastici*. Mario Broglio begins to buy his works and make them known.
Meeting with Carrà, who visits his studio.
Visits Raimondi in Rome and is introduced to de Chirico and the literary figures associated with the magazine *La Ronda*. Embarks with Raimondi on a study of the works by Caravaggio in the churches and the museums of Rome.

1920
Visits the Venice Biennale and sees the room devoted to Cézanne in the French Pavilion. Returns to etching for the first time since 1915.

1921
Exhibits works together with Carrà, de Chirico, Arturo Martini, Melli, and Zadkine in Berlin at the first show of the Valori Plastici group, organized by Mario Broglio.

1922
Takes part with de Chirico, Carrà, and Arturo Martini in the exhibition *Fiorentina Primaverile* in Florence. Presented in the catalogue by Giorgio de Chirico.

1926
Exhibits three paintings in the *Prima Mostra del Novecento* at the Palazzo della Permanente in Milan. One-year appointment as director of the elementary schools of some small towns in the provinces of Modena and Reggio Emilia.

1927
Spends the summer at Grizzana in the Emilian Apennines, where he was to return every summer until 1932. Devotes more time to etching.

1928
Exhibits some etchings at the XVI Venice Biennale. A short autobiographical sketch appears in the Bolognese magazine *L'Assalto*.
Articles written on his work by Mino Maccari and Leo Longanesi.

1929
Exhibits three paintings, three etchings, and two drawings at the *Seconda Mostra del Novecento* in Milan.

1930
Assigned the chair in etching at the Bologna Accademia di Belle Arti on the grounds of acknowledged distinction (position held until 1956). Exhibits three paintings, two etchings, and a portfolio of engravings at the XVII Venice Biennale.
Takes part in an exhibition of etching at the Bibliothèque Nationale de France in Paris.

1931
Exhibits three paintings and some etchings at the I Rome Quadriennale.

1932
Takes part in the *Prima Mostra dell'Incisione Italiana Moderna* in Florence. A special issue of Leo Longanesi's magazine *L'Italiano* is devoted to him with an essay by Ardengo Soffici and numerous reproductions of paintings, etchings, and drawings.

1934
Exhibits two etchings at the XIX Venice Biennale. Acclaimed as "one of the best Italian painters alive" by Roberto Longhi in a celebrated inaugural lecture at Bologna University in November.

1935
Exhibits four paintings and two etchings at the II Rome Quadriennale. Takes part in an exhibition of ancient and modern Italian art in Paris.

1937
Takes part in an exhibition of Italian art in Berlin.

1938
Takes part in an exhibition of Italian art in Berne. Proposed by Ardengo Soffici and accepted as corresponding member of the Accademia delle Arti del Disegno – the oldest Italian academy, founded in Florence by Giorgio Vasari in 1563 – on October 15.

1939
Exhibits forty-two paintings, nine etchings, and two drawings in a personal room at the III Rome Quadriennale. Awarded the second prize for painting, with the first going to Bruno Saetti. Sends paintings to the Golden Gate International Exhibition of Contemporary Art in San Francisco and the Carnegie Prize in Pittsburgh. An essay by Cesare Brandi appears in *Le Arti* and Arnaldo Beccaria publishes his first monographic study on the artist.
Returns in the summer to Grizzana, where he was subsequently to spend long periods painting in the summer months.

1940
Takes part in an exhibition of Italian art in Zurich.

1942
The art historian Cesare Brandi publishes an important monographic study.

1943
Takes part in the IV Rome Quadriennale. Forced by the war to leave Bologna and take refuge in Grizzana, where he remains until July 25, 1944. Paints numerous landscapes during this period.

1945
Solo show of twenty-one paintings at the Il Fiore gallery in Florence, immediately after the city's liberation by the Allies. Organized by Roberto Longhi, the author of the very important presentation, and held in April, when the artist was still cut off in Bologna and there was no news of his fate.
Show of fifty paintings organized by Pier Maria Bardi at the Studio d'Arte Palma in Rome.

1947
Appointed member of the figurative arts committee set up to organize the important event of the first Venice Biennale to be held after a break of six years in 1948. This would be an opportunity for the artist to have international artistic contacts and a direct understanding of the facts.

1948
Exhibits eleven paintings at the XXIX Venice Biennale in the group show *Tre Pittori Italiani Dal 1910 al 1920*, together with Carrà and de Chirico. Awarded the prize of the City of Venice for an Italian painter by an international jury. Made

a member of the Accademia Nazionale di San Luca in Rome.
Exhibition of eighty-eight etchings presented by Carlo Alberto Petrucci at the Calcografia Nazionale in Rome.

1949
Exhibits thirteen paintings and five etchings at the major exhibition *Twentieth-century Italian Art* organized by James Thrall Soby and Alfred Barr at the Museum of Modern Art in New York. Solo show of graphic works organized by Giuseppe Raimondi at the Musée des Beaux-Arts in Brussels.

1950
Takes part in *L'Art Italien moderne* at the Musée National d'Art Moderne in Paris and *Modern Italian Art* at the Tate Gallery in London. Awarded a prize at the *International Exhibition of Black and White* in Lugano.

1952
Exhibits one work in the major exhibition *La nature morte de l'antiquité à nos jours* at the Orangerie in Paris, curated by Charles Sterling. Made a member of the Swedish Academy.

1953
Exhibits twenty-five etchings at the II Bienal de São Paulo Museum of Modern Art.
Awarded the first prize for etching.

1954
Survey exhibition of fifty-nine paintings and forty-three etchings organized by Vitale Bloch and Lamberto Vitali and held first at the Gemeentemuseum in the Hague and then at the New Burlington Galleries in London.

1955
Exhibits seven paintings at the VII Rome Quadriennale. First solo show at the Delius Gallery in New York. Interview with Professor Peppino Mangravite of Columbia University, subsequently broadcasted by the Voice of America radio station in 1957.

1956
Goes to Winterthur for a solo show of fiftysix paintings, four drawings, and forty etchings at the Kunstmuseum, alongside works by Giacomo Manzù. Visits the collection of Oskar Reinhart.

1957
Exhibits thirty paintings in the "Sala Especial" organized by the Venice Biennale at the IV Bienal de São Paulo with an introduction in the catalogue by Rodolfo Pallucchini. Awarded the first prize for painting ahead of Marc Chagall.
Exhibits six paintings and six etchings in an exhibition *Arte Italiana dal 1910* at the Grosse Kunstausstellung in Munich.
Solo show of thirty-five paintings, two watercolors, ten drawings, and thirteen etchings at the World House Galleries in New York, presented by Lionello Venturi.
General catalogue *L'opera grafica* drawn up by Lamberto Vitali.

1958
Important interview with Edouard Roditi, published in 1960.
Exhibits twelve etchings at the V International Exhibition of Black and White in Lugano.

1960
Another solo show held at the World House Galleries in New York.

1962
Solo show of nineteen paintings and thirteen etchings at the Haus Seel am Markt in Siegen, Germany. Awarded the city's Rubens Prize for painting.
Made an honorary member of the Accademia delle Arti del Disegno in Florence.

1963
Awarded the Archiginnasio d'Oro prize by the City of Bologna. Solo show of forty-one paintings, seven drawings, and sixty-five etchings at the Galerie Krugier in Geneva.

1964
Monographic study by Lamberto Vitali published in January. Last *Natura morta* (V. 1342) signed in February.
Dies on June 18.
Important monographic study by Francesco Arcangeli published in July.

Quoted bibliography

General information

For the works of Giorgio Morandi, it is indicated, in each occasion, the general catalogues and the corresponding publications' edition with the following abbreviations:

V. and the corresponding catalogue's edition
L. Vitali, *Morandi. Catalogo generale*, Electa, Milan, 1977, 2 voll. (II ed. extended, 1983)

V. inc. and the corresponding catalogue's edition
L. Vitali, *Giorgio Morandi. Opera grafica*, Einaudi, Turin, 1957 (II ed. extended and corrected, 1964; III ed. extended and corrected, 1978; IV ed. extended, 1989)

P. and the corresponding catalogue's edition
M. Pasquali, *Morandi. Acquerelli. Catalogo generale*, Electa, Milan, 1991

T. P. and the corresponding catalogue's edition
E. Tavoni, M. Pasquali, *Morandi. Disegni. Catalogo generale*, Electa, Milan, 1994

P.2000 and the corresponding catalogue number for the paintings (for the watercolors it is preceded by an A and for drawings by a D)
M. Pasquali, *Morandi. Opere catalogate tra il 1985 e il 2000*, Museo Morandi – Musica Insieme, Bologna, 2000

R. Longhi, *Piero della Francesca*, Edition for *Valori Plastici*, Rome 1927.

G. Morandi in his own autobiography "Giorgio Morandi" in *Autobiografie di scrittori e di artisti*, in "L'Assalto", 18th February 1928.

R. Longhi, "Momenti della pittura bolognese", in *L'Archiginnasio*, 1-3, 1935, p. 135.

G. Morandi to P. Bargellini, "Artisti italiani: Giorgio Morandi", *Il Frontespizio*, September 1937.

C. Brandi, "Cammino di Morandi", in *Le Arti*, n. 3, Rome, February-March 1939.

R. Longhi, *Giorgio Morandi*, exhibition catalogue (Florence, Il Fiore Galleria d'arte moderna, 21 April – 3 May 1945), Florence, 1945.

O. Stonorov, C. L. Ragghianti (edited by), *Mostra di Frank Lloyd Wright: catalogo itinerario*, exhibition catalogue (Philadelphia, Gimbel Brother Department Store, 27 January – 25 February 1951; Florence, Palazzo Strozzi, 24 June – September 1951), Edizioni di Comunità, Rome, 1951.

Arte moderna in una raccolta italiana, exhibition catalogue (Florence, La Strozzina, April – May 1953), Edizioni del Milione, Milan, 1953, pp. 12-17.

C. L. Ragghianti, "Giorgio Morandi", in *La Critica d'Arte*, I, January 1954, p. 50.

P. P. Pasolini, "Presentazione", in *Irene Brin e Gaspero Del Corso le Annunciano l'inaugurazione della mostra di Renzo Vespignani*, exhibition catalogue (Rome, Galleria L'Obelisco, 16 November 1956).

L. Vitali, *Giorgio Morandi. Opera grafica,* Einaudi, Turin, 1957 (II expanded and corrected ed., 1964; III expanded and corrected ed., 1978; IV expanded ed., 1989).

R. Longhi, "Avvertenze per il lettore", in *Scritti giovanili 1912-1922*, (*Opere complete,* I, 1), Florence, 1961, pp. X-XI.

A. Bertolucci, "Un maestro explosivo", in *L'Illustrazione Italiana*, December 1962, p. 62.

F. Arcangeli, *Giorgio Morandi*, Umberto Allemandi, Milan, 1964.

R. Longhi, *Exit Morandi*, pronounced speech for the televisual "L'Approdo" broadcast on 28 June 1964 and printed in *L'Approdo letterario*, X, 26 April – June 1964, pp. 3-4.

Catalogo della XXXIII Esposizione Biennale Internazionale d'Arte Biennale di Venezia, exhibition catalogue (Venice, Palazzo Centrale, 18 June – 16 October 1966), Venice, 1966.

R. Longhi, "Giorgio Morandi", preface to "Mostra Personale di Giorgio Morandi", in *Catalogo della XXXIII Esposizione Biennale Internazionale d'Arte*, exhibition catalogue (Venice, Palazzo Centrale, 18th June-16th October 1966), Venice, 1966, p. 22.

C. L. Ragghianti (edited by), *Arte moderna in Italia 1915-1935*, exhibition catalogue (Florence, Palazzo Strozzi, 26 February – 28 May 1967), Marchi e Bertolli Editori, Florence, 1967.

La raccolta Alberto Della Ragione, Museo d'Arte Contemporanea di Firenze, exhibition catalogue and bibliography by R. Monti and F. Ragghianti, Cassa di Risparmio di Firenze, Centro Di, Florence, 1970.

C. Brandi, *Morandi lungo il cammino*, Rizzoli, Milan, 1970.

C. L. Ragghianti, *Arte, fare e vedere dall'arte al museo*, Vallecchi, Florence, 1974, p. 111.

L. Vitali, *Morandi. Catalogo generale*, Electa, Milan, 1977, 2 voll. (II expanded ed., 1983).

R. Longhi, *Da Cimabue a Morandi. Saggi di storia della pittura italiana scelti e ordinati da Gianfranco Contini*, Arnoldo Mondadori, Milan, 1973, p. 217.

C. L. Ragghianti, "Morandi o l'architettura della visione", in Id., *Bologna cruciale 1914 e saggi su Morandi, Gorni, Saetti*, (Opere di C. L. Ragghianti, VIII) Calderini, Bologna, 1982, pp. 22-253.

R. Longhi, *Scritti sull'Otto e Novecento 1925-1966*, (*Opere complete* XIV), Sansoni, Florence, 1984.

C. L. Ragghianti, "Geometria di Morandi", in *La Nazione*, third page, Tuesday 8 April 1985.

C. L. Ragghianti, "Piante di Morandi", in *Critica d'Arte*, fourth series, LI, 10, July-September 1986, pp. 23-24.

F. Scalia (edited by), *Raccolta d'Arte Contemporanea Alberto Della Ragione*, Centro Di, Florence, 1987.

M. Pasquali, *Morandi. Acquerelli. Catalogo generale*, Electa, Milan, 1991.

C. Sisi (edited by), *Da Fattori a Burri. Dipinti, sculture e disegni dalla Collezione della Banca Toscana,* exhibition catalogue (Florence, Museo Marino Marini, 6 April – 24 May 1993), Centro Di, Florence, 1993.

E. Tavoni, M. Pasquali, *Morandi. Disegni. Catalogo generale*, Electa, Milan, 1994.

P. Mandelli, "Storia di una monografia", in *Accademia Clementina – Atti e Memorie*, n. 35-36, Bologna, 1995-1996, pp. 333-334.

M. Heidegger, *Sentieri interrotti*, translation by P. Chiodi, La Nuova Italia, Florence, 1996.

A. Vettese, "Morandi e la cultura artistica del secondo dopoguerra", in L. Mattioli Rossi (edited by), *Morandi ultimo. Nature morte 1950-1964*, exhibition catalogue (Verona, Galleria dello Scudo, 14 December 1997 – 28 February 1998; then Venice, Peggy Guggenheim Collection, 30 April – 13 September 1998), Mazzotta, Milan, 1997, pp. 59-68.

C. Brandi, *Come un'autobiografia*, edited by V. Rubiu, Edizioni della Cometa, Rome, 1998.

M. Pasquali, *Morandi. Opere catalogate tra il 1985 e il 2000*, Museo Morandi – Musica Insieme, Bologna, 2000.

M. C. Bandera, "Prefazione", in *Morandi sceglie Morandi. Corrispondenza con la Biennale 1947-1962*, Charta, Milan, 2001.

M. Gregori, "Longhi tra antico e moderno", in C. Spadoni (edited by), *Da Renoir a De Staël. Roberto Longhi e il moderno*, exhibition catalogue (Ravenna, Loggetta Lombardesca, 23 February – 30 June 2003), Mazzotta, Milan, 2003, p. 16.

M. C. Bandera (edited by), *Morandi e Firenze. I suoi amici critici e collezionisti*, exhibition catalogue (Florence, Fondazione di Studi di Storia dell'Arte Roberto Longhi, 21 January – 6 March 2005), Mazzotta, Milan, 2005, pp. 15-35.

M. C. Bandera, "Morandi e Firenze. I suoi amici critici e collezionisti", in M. C. Bandera (edited by), *Morandi e Firenze. I suoi amici critici e collezionisti*, exhibition catalogue (Florence, Fondazione di Studi di Storia dell'Arte Roberto Longhi, 21 January – 6 March 2005), Mazzotta, Milan, 2005.

M. C. Bandera, Morandi e Firenze. I suoi amici critici e collezionisti, exhibition catalogue (Florence, Fondazione di Studi di Storia dell'Arte Roberto Longhi, 21 January – 6 March 2005), Mazzotta, Milan, 2005.

M. C. Bandera, "Miscellanea per Morandi", in *Paragone*, LVII, 67 (675), May 2006, pp. 43-46.

S. Pollack (director), *Sketches of Frank Gehry*, documentary film produced by Ultan Guilfoyle, United States, 2006.

P. Coldwell, *Morandi's Legacy. Influences in British Art*, exhibition catalogue (Kendall, Abbott Hall, 12 January – 25 March 2006; London, Estorick Collection of Modern Italian Art, 5 April – 18 June 2006), Wilson, London, 2006.

A. M. Guiducci, "La villa di Cesare Brandi a Vignano: una donazione allo Stato", in L. Fornari Schianchi, A. M. Guiducci (edited by), *La passione e l'arte. Cesare Brandi e Luigi Magnani collezionisti*, exhibition catalogue (Siena, Complesso Museale di Santa Maria della Scala – Palazzo Squarcialupi, 8 December 2006 – 11 March 2007), Umberto Allemandi, Turin, 2006, pp. 23-29.

S. Scully, *Resistance and Persistence: Selected Writings*, edited by F. Ingleby, Merrell Publishers, London, 2006 and republished in S. Scully, *Inner: The Collected Writings and Selected Interviews of Sean Scully*, Hatje Cantz, Berlin, 2016.

M. C. Bandera, "Longhi e gli amici pittori", in M. Gregori e G. Romano (edited by), *La collezione di Roberto Longhi dal Duecento a Caravaggio a Morandi*, exhibition catalogue (Alba, Fondazione Ferrero, 14 October 2007 – 10 February 2008), L'Artistica Editrice, Savigliano (Cuneo), 2007.

L. Cesari (edited by), *Giorgio Morandi di Francesco Arcangeli. Stesura originaria inedita. Introduzione, apparati, note*, Umberto Allemandi, Turin, 2007.

D. DeLillo, *Falling Man*, Scribner, New York, 2007.

C. Brandi, *Morandi*, edited by M. Pasquali, Gli Ori, Pistoia, 2008.

D. DeLillo, *L'uomo che cade*, Einaudi, Turin, 2008.

R. Longhi, *Da Cimabue a Morandi*, Arnoldo Mondadori, Milan, 2008.

M. C. Bandera, R. Miracco (edited by), *Giorgio Morandi 1890-1964*, exhibition catalogue (New York, The Metropolitan Museum of Art, 16 September – 14 December 2008; Bologna, MAMbo – Museo d'Arte Moderna di Bologna, 22 January – 13 April 2009), Skira, Milan, 2008.

G. Maraniello (edited by) *Bernd & Hilla Becher at Museo Morandi*, exhibition catalogue (Bologna, Museo Morandi, 24 January – 19 April 2009).

P. Auster, *Sunset Park*, Einaudi, Turin, 2010.

M. Pasquali, S. Bulgarelli (edited by), *Tre voci. Carlo L. Ragghianti, Cesare Gnudi, Giorgio Morandi*, Gli Ori, Pistoia, 2010.

M. Franciolli, "Assonanze", in M. C. Bandera, M. Franciolli (edited by), *Giorgio Morandi*, exhibition catalogue (Lugano, Museo d'Arte Città di Lugano, 10 March – 1 July 2012), Silvana Editoriale, Cinisello Balsamo (Milan), 2012, pp. 200-213.

B. Schwabsky, "Giorgio Morandi. Center For Fine Arts, Brussels", in *Artforum*, October 2013, pp. 290-291.

F. Fergonzi, "Morandi e i quadri degli altri", in *Filologia del 900 Modigliani Sironi Morandi Martini*, Electa, Milan, 2013, pp. 161-216.

M. C. Bandera, "Giorgio Morandi: Modern Restlessness", in Ead. (edited by), *Giorgio Morandi. A retrospective*, exhibition catalogue (Bruxelles, Bozar – Palais des Beaux-Arts, 6 June – 22 September 2013), Silvana Editoriale, Cinisello Balsamo (Milan), 2013, pp. 13-44.

C. Brandi, "Cammino di Morandi", 1939, in V. Rubiu Brandi (edited by), *Scritti d'arte*, Milan, 2013, pp. 623-659.

C. Brandi, *Morandi lungo il cammino*, edited by V. Rubiu Brandi, Castelvecchi, Rome, 2014.

G. Maraniello (edited by), *Rachel Whiteread. Study for Room*, exhibition catalogue (Bologna, MAMbo – Museo d'Arte Moderna di Bologna, 24 January – 4 May 2014), Bologna, 2014.

Z. Fanzhi, "Voglio che la mia Cina s'innamori di Morandi", in *Sette – Corriere della Sera*, 12, 21 March 2014.

M. C. Bandera, *Quaderni della collezione Merlini 2*, in M. C. Bandera (edited by), *Giorgio Morandi Roberto Longhi. Opere Lettere Scritti*, exhibition catalogue (Florence, Fondazione di Studi di Storia dell'Arte Roberto Longhi, 1 June – 22 June 2014), Silvana Editoriale, Cinisello Balsamo (Milan), 2014.

M. C. Bandera, "Morandi's Eye. From Giotto to Piero della Francesca, Caravaggio, Zurbarán and Vermeer", in L. Selleri e G. Vecchi (edited by), *Morandi infinite variations*, exhibition catalogue (Hyogo, Prefectural Museum of Art, 8 December 2015 – 14 February 2016; Tokyo, Station Gallery, 20 February – 10 April 2016; Iwate Museum, 16 April – 5 June 2016), Tokyo, 2015, pp.14-23 and 170-176.

M. C. Bandera, "Giorgio Morandi: la ricerca dell'essenza", in M. C. Bandera (edited by), *Giorgio Morandi*, exhibition catalogue (Rome, Complesso del Vittoriano, 28 February – 21 June 2015), Skira, Milan, 2015, pp. 44-45.

Y. Bonnefoy, *Morandi, Giacometti e Hollan*, Abscondita, Milan, 2015.

M. C. Bandera, "Sotto il segno di Cézanne. Il nodo Longhi – Morandi – Piero della Francesca", in A. Paolucci, D. Benati, F. Dabell, F. Mazzocca, P. Refice, U. Tramonti (edited by), *Piero della Francesca. Indagine su un mito*, exhibition catalogue (Forlì, Musei San Domenico, 13 February – 26 June 2016), Silvana Editoriale, Cinisello Balsamo (Milan), 2016, pp. 331-332.

M. Recalcati, *Il mistero delle cose. Nove ritratti di artisti*, Feltrinelli, Milan, 2016.

M. Maiorino, "1964-2018: Morandi dopo Morandi", in *Il dispositivo Morandi. Arte e critica 1934- 2018*, introduction by S. Zuliani, Quodlibet, Macerata, 2019, pp. 109-194.

M. C. Bandera, "Morandi, Roberto Longhi e gli Old Masters", in P. Joos (edited by), *A Backward Glance: Giorgio Morandi and the Old Masters*, exhibition catalogue (Bilbao, Guggenheim Bilbao, 12 April – 6 October 2019), in process of publication.

Exit Morandi

Museo Novecento Firenze
15 March - 27 June 2019

EXHIBITION PROMOTED BY
Comune di Firenze

IN COLLABORATION WITH
Fondazione di Studi
di Storia dell'Arte
Roberto Longhi, Firenze

CONCEPT AND SCIENTIFIC
DIRECTION
Sergio Risaliti

CURATED BY
Maria Cristina Bandera
and Sergio Risaliti

ORGANIZATION AND COORDINATION
Eva Francioli, Francesca Neri,
Stefania Rispoli - MUS.E
Luca Puri

COMMUNICATION
MUS.E

PRESS OFFICE
Elisa Di Lupo,
Comune di Firenze
Daniele Pasquini,
MUS.E
Ludovica V. Zarrilli,
Tabloid soc coop

VISUAL IDENTITY
Concept:
FRUSH design studio
Realization:
Dania Menafra

HANDLING AND
ART WORKS PREPARATION
APICE FIRENZE s.r.l.
ARTERÌA s.r.l.

CONDITION REPORT
Debora Minotti

RESTORATIONS ARTWORKS FROM
FONDAZIONE ROBERTO LONGHI
Studio 4 Restauro Dipinti

INSURANCE
Strategica Group

TRANSLATIONS
Frank Dabell for texts
by Maria Cristina Bandera
NTL – Il Nuovo
Traduttore Letterario

CATALOGUE
Forma Edizioni

EXHIBITION PHOTOGRAPHS
Leonardo Morfini

ARTWORKS PHOTOGRAPHS
Fototeca Musei Civici Fiorentini
Foto Lensini, Siena
Foto Pinacoteca Nazionale di Siena,
Archivio Cesare Brandi,
su concessione del Ministero
dei Beni e delle Attività Culturali.
Polo Museale della Toscana
Foto Archivio Pinacoteca
Nazionale di Siena. Su concessione
del Ministero dei Beni e delle Attività
Culturali. Polo Museale della Toscana
Foto Galleria Nazionale d'Arte
Moderna e Contemporanea, Roma
Claudio Giusti per Fondazione
Roberto Longhi

COVER IMAGE
Natura morta (natura morta
di oggetti in viola), 1937, detail.
Fondazione di studi di Soria dell'Arte
Roberto Longhi, Firenze

GRAPHIC PRINTS ON DISPLAY
Litografia Ip srls

A SPECIAL THANK TO THE LENDERS
OF THE ARTWORKS
Collezione Banca Monte dei Paschi di Siena
Collezione Gori, Pistoia
Collezione Merlini, Busto Arsizio (VA)
Elisabetta Fabbri e Franco Faldi
Fondazione di Studi di Storia
dell'Arte Roberto Longhi, Florence
Galleria Nazionale d'Arte Moderna
e Contemporanea, Rome
Carlo e Rosella Nesi
Polo Museale della Toscana,
Collezione Cesare Brandi, Vignano

and the collectors who prefer
to stay private

THANKS TO
Rosa Alba Acquaviva, Laura Andreini,
Lorenzo Balbi,Gabriele Bartalucci,
Marta Bellaveglia, Andrea Bianchi,
Stefano Casciu, Elena Chiti,
Saretto Cincinelli, Cristiana Collu,
Daniela De Palma, Laura Doretto,
Marcello Fallaci, Francesco Fricelli,
Mariella Gnani, Cristina Gnoni Mavarelli,
Giuliano Gori, Andrea Jengo, Carlo Lisi,
Miranda MacPhail, Maria Mangiavacchi,
Stefano Marson, Alessia Masi, Maria Maugeri,
Giuseppe Merlini, Museo Morandi Bologna,
Ambra Nepi, Antonella Nesi, Letizia Nesi,
Antonella Nicola, Daniela Nozzoli,
Daniele Rapino, Ana Redondo Plaza,
Rai Teche, Felicia Rotundo, Lorenza Selleri,
Lapo Sergi, Matteo Spanò, Luca Toni,
Giusi Vecchi, Margherita Viola

TECHNICAL SPONSOR
Forma Edizioni
Litografia Ip Srls
Strategica Group

**Fondazione di Studi di Storia
dell'Arte Roberto Longhi, Firenze**

Forma Edizioni Srl

Florence, Italy

redazione@formaedizioni.it
www.formaedizioni.it

EDITORIAL DIRECTION
Laura Andreini

EDITORIAL CONSULTANT
Riccardo Bruscagli

EDITORIAL STAFF
Maria Giulia Caliri
Livia D'Aliasi
Andrea Benelli

GRAPHIC DESIGN
Elisa Balducci

PHOTOLITOGRAPHY
LAB di Gallotti
Giuseppe Fulvio
Florence, Italy

First edition: March 2019

This volume was printed by
Tap Grafiche, Poggibonsi (SI), Italy